THE REFERENCE SHELF   VOLUME 43 NUMBER 4

REPRESENTATIVE AMERICAN SPEECHES: 1970-1971

EDITED BY WALDO W. BRADEN

Professor of Speech
Louisiana State University

THE H. W. WILSON COMPANY

NEW YORK   1971

THE REFERENCE SHELF

The books in this series contain reprints of articles, excerpts from books, and addresses on current issues and social trends in the United States and other countries. There are six separately bound numbers in each volume, all of which are generally published in the same calendar year. One number is a collection of recent speeches; each of the others is devoted to a single subject and gives background information and discussion from various points of view, concluding with a comprehensive bibliography. Books in the series may be purchased individually or on subscription.

REPRESENTATIVE AMERICAN SPEECHES: 1970-1971

Copyright © 1971

By The H. W. Wilson Company

International Standard Book Number 0-8242-0449-2
Library of Congress Catalog Card Number (38-27962)

PRINTED IN THE UNITED STATES OF AMERICA

PREFACE

In opening his debate with Robert Y. Hayne, Daniel Webster said: "When the mariner has been tossed for many days in thick weather, and on an unknown sea, he naturally avails himself of the first pause in the storm, the earliest glance of the sun, to take his latitude, and ascertain how far the elements have driven him from his true course." Let me "imitate this prudence" in this preface and make some observations about the state of the rhetorical idiom in 1970-1971.

The political speaking has been uninspiring and ephemeral. The fall campaign produced much heat but little light. Taking an unusually active part in the canvass, President Nixon and Vice President Agnew stressed law and order rather than the crucial issues of foreign policy and the economic recession. The Vice President strove energetically to unseat Democrats and liberal Republicans in a campaign which was only partially successful. In key states, particularly Illinois, Texas, New York, California, and Indiana, senatorial campaigns were directed at least in part by public relations experts who put more faith in thirty- and sixty-second radio and TV spots than in speeches. Key political figures such as Edmund S. Muskie, Edward M. Kennedy, Hubert H. Humphrey, Nelson A. Rockefeller, and John V. Lindsay did almost no speaking outside their home states.

On November 1, 1970, James Reston of the New York *Times* noted that not a single campaign speech on either side had been printed in full in a major newspaper. He further observed: "The campaign . . . has diverted the attention of the people from the fundamental issues of poverty, unemployment, race, disarmament and war to the issues of party personality, ideology and the savage opposition of the young militants" (New York *Times,* November 1, 1970). The night before the election, the liberal Democrats, smarting from the sting of the Vice President's rhetoric, prevailed upon Muskie to deliver on nationwide television a speech put together by several collaborators.

If 1970-1971 is a weathervane, it may be that significant deliberative speaking in the public forum and in Congress is on the wane. If so, it may be because the mass media have become so expensive and so complex that only the rich can afford to use them to reach the voters. To win the governorship of New York in 1970, Rockefeller is reported to have spent more than six million dollars and to have utilized a staff of 370 full-time employees. Special interests seem to reduce political speaking to appeals to the lowest common element, with emphasis upon turning out the vote while offending as few listeners as possible. Stereotypes, slogans, and signal responses are substituted for reasoned discourse. In the legislative halls, decisions concerning important legislation are too often made in committees and votes reflect pressure from large power blocs, impervious to anything so fragile as oratorical persuasion.

Speaking in Congress, likewise, was inconsequential. Petty bickering and filibustering occupied much of the time of the lawmakers. While the two parties maneuvered for political advantage, important legislation never reached the floor. At the close of the Ninety-first Congress, Senate Majority Leader Mike Mansfield (Democrat, Montana) said, "I am disturbed at the image which this body is showing to the nation, but I am more disturbed at the image we are showing to ourselves." Appraising the situation, President Nixon observed: "We are all talking. . . . We are having press conferences. We are on TV. We are making speeches and we aren't thinking enough about it. That is why there are so few great speeches. That is why there are so few great thinkers."

On the other hand, college and university audiences have attracted a variety of speakers. Kingman Brewster, Jr., president of Yale, has called "the campus an oasis of tolerance in a desert of mistrust." He continued, "The chance to pursue the good, the true, and the beautiful seems today in even sharper contrast to the ugliness of the outer world. The broad scope of personal freedom to probe and to experiment is still a special privilege of student youth."

The controversial list of sixty-five alleged "radical and/or revolutionary speakers" compiled and publicized by Representative Richard H. Ichord (Democrat, Missouri), Chairman of the House Internal Security Committee, provides evidence that the campus is probably the freest forum in the nation. Representative Ichord also suggested that colleges offer financial support to speakers who otherwise might not be heard outside their local spheres.

Increasing numbers of prominent political figures journeyed to campuses to give some of their better speeches. Worried about student alienation, President Nixon took time to speak at Kansas State University, September 15, 1970, and at the University of Nebraska, January 14, 1971. Frank Church, Democratic Senator from Idaho, spoke on "Foreign Policy and the Generation Gap" at Washington University and later on "Let Us Come Together" at Johns Hopkins University. Senator J. William Fulbright (Democrat, Arkansas), spoke at the University of South Florida on "The Legislator: Congress and the War." Retired Chief Justice Earl Warren appeared at Kansas State University speaking on "The Alternative Is Chaos"; Senator Ernest F. Hollings of South Carolina (Democrat) spoke to the Blue Key Society at the University of Georgia; Mike Mansfield discussed "The Nixon Doctrine" at Olivet College in Michigan on March 28. Arthur F. Burns, chairman of the Federal Reserve Board discussed how to fight inflation and extend prosperity at Pepperdine College on December 8. John D. Rockefeller III addressed students at Amherst College, and Senate Minority Leader Hugh Scott (Republican, Pennsylvania) was invited to speak at Kansas State on "Implications of Foreign Policy."

Why do public figures make some of their better speeches to university and college audiences? The answer may be at least twofold. First, they rise to the challenge of facing critical listeners, who demand more and who may talk back.

Second, some may feel more at ease in the academic atmosphere with more homogeneous listeners and without the pressures of cynical Washington correspondents, curious tourists, and bored colleagues. In other words, they respond to the "campus as an oasis of tolerance." It is to be hoped that, unlike Representative Ichord, other political figures will realize the importance of keeping this platform free and unhampered. But name-calling, attempted blacklisting, efforts by politicians to provoke campus violence and attempts by obnoxious students to create disturbance and to shout down those with whom they disagree could doom this fragile forum.

Throughout the year, the subject of youth and its alienation was a popular topic. In a speech entitled "Youth and the Establishment: Can They Work Together?" delivered at Amherst College, John D. Rockefeller III isolated the issue in this question: "Is it possible for youth and the Establishment to come together to break through misunderstandings, the anger and hostility which now divides them?" His disjunctive absolutes suggested the seriousness of the problem.

With the opening of the school year, college and university officials feared the resumption of the confrontations of the previous year. Their anxiety stirred many to deliver thoughtful and carefully prepared convocation speeches at the opening of the school term. Worthy of note were the speeches of John H. Bunzel of San Jose State College, John A. Flowers of Kent State University, Robert D. Clark of the University of Oregon, W. Allen Wallis of the University of Rochester, Clifford L. Lord of Hofstra University, Oswald Tippo of the University of Massachusetts, George Dana Brabson of Ohio Northern University, John A. Howard of Rockford College, and Theodore M. Hesburgh of the University of Notre Dame. Tau Kappa Alpha-Delta Sigma Rho selected President Robert D. Clark as its Speaker of the Year.

Just as the politicians were sought for campus addresses, so college administrators found attentive listeners among business and professional men. Dr. Eric A. Walker, retired president of Pennsylvania State University, discussed "High Education Faces Real Disaster" before the Traffic Club of Pittsburgh, January 28, 1971. In what must be the most pessimistic talk of the year on youth, Dr. Edward Teller of the University of California at Berkeley found a similarity between the pre-Hitler Brownshirts and the New Left (*Congressional Record*, April 21, 1971, page E 3295). Kingman Brewster, Jr., president of Yale, discussed the generation gap in a speech entitled "The Deeper Unrest," December 6, 1970, before the Ford Hall Forum, Boston. Dr. William McGill, the new president of Columbia University, gave some unusually perceptive speeches on youth before the American Institute of Banking in New York City, February 6, 1971, and before the Economic Club of Detroit, February 16, 1971. The latter speech (see *Vital Speeches of the Day*, March 15, 1971, pages 337-40), an analysis of the causes of the social ferment, deserves a wide reading.

Vice President Spiro T. Agnew continued to stir what Lester Thonssen in the last volume of REPRESENTATIVE AMERICAN SPEECHES: 1969-1970 (page 60) called "instantaneous, often acerbic and . . . unremitting response from his opposition." During the fall campaign he denounced the broadcasting of rock music. Nicholas Johnson, the most outspoken member of the Federal Communications Commission, replied in several speeches. In a speech entitled "Government by Television: A Case Study, Perspective and Proposals" before the International Association of Political Consultants, December 14, 1970, Johnson presented an exhaustive analysis of the Administration attempt to use television in influencing the American people. After presentation by the Columbia Broadcasting System of a news special "The Selling of the Pentagon," February 23, 1971, Vice President Agnew resumed his attack on the media. Before the Middlesex Club of Boston, March 18, 1971, he accused CBS of bias and unethical editing. Sensitive to criticism from any quarter, radio and television personalities answered the Vice President in kind, countering that the Administraton was attempting to intimidate television news reporters and was violating the freedom of the press guaranteed under the First Amendment. At this writing the controversy promises to become even more bitter with the underlying issues involving how this powerful medium is to be used in a free society.

The previous paragraphs suggest some trends in the public address of the year and mention some speeches that could have been included in this volume had space permitted. The New York *Times, Vital Speeches of the Day,* the *Congressional Record,* and other periodicals and newspapers continue to provide the interested student of the rhetorical idiom numerous speeches for reading, study, analysis, and reflection. They suggest that ours is an oral society and that speakers have much to say on many issues.

Reacting to current demands for relevance in scholarship and education, Harvard history professor Oscar Handlin, recently argued that "a scholar who takes his signals from the headlines is doomed. . . . Chasing from one disaster to another, he loses sight of the long-term trend; busy with the Band-Aid, he has no time to trace the patient's health." A similar danger exists for the compiler of a collection of speeches. The editor of this volume has indeed been tested in attempting to select representative discourses from the mass of speech texts that have crossed his desk. In rereading the introductions of his two distinguished predecessors, the present editor now realizes why they modestly reiterated on several occasions that in the final sense what they included in their selections was based upon personal judgments—yes, their preferences.

The present editor does not claim to have found a better method, or developed any keener sense, or superior insight than those of his two mentors. What appears in the 1970-1971 volume again represents what seems to have substance and worth at the moment. The point of view of the present editor is similar to that of the two previous ones, to whom he owes much and is deeply indebted on many counts.

He is much in the debt of many others who have assisted him in assembling and editing this volume. His research assistant, Mrs. Barbara Walsh, has been extremely helpful in locating and preparing materials. Valuable suggestions have come from his colleagues in the Department of Speech at Louisiana State University: Owen Peterson, Stephen Cooper, Harold Mixon, J. Donald Ragsdale, Francine Merritt, Mary Frances Hopkins, and Clinton Bradford. Help has also come from Bower Aly, Charles Balcer, Bert Bradley, Robert Jeffrey, Mary Margaret Roberts, Mary Louise Gehring, Horace G. Rahskopf, and Robert W. Smith. Of course, the volume could never have appeared without the help of the editor's secretaries: Carolyn Russell and Linda Michelli.

WALDO W. BRADEN

Baton Rouge, Louisiana
August 1971

CONTENTS

COURT REFORM

STATE OF THE JUDICIARY [1]

WARREN E. BURGER [2]

The campaign for law and order, the resignation of Abe Fortas, the criticism of the Warren Court, the congressional refusal to approve Clement F. Haynsworth and G. Harrold Carswell (two of President Nixon's nominees to the High Court), the criticism of Justice William O. Douglas, and most recently the revelations concerning prison conditions (for example, see *Newsweek,* March 8, 1971), have intensified public interest in the courts and particularly the Supreme Court. President Nixon, Vice President Agnew, and Attorney General Mitchell have pressed hard for "law and order" and have pledged to rearm the "peace forces" against the "criminal forces." Of course, President Nixon's appointments of Warren E. Burger as chief justice and Harry A. Blackmun as an associate justice were intended to check the liberal drift of the Court and to appease conservatives. In this climate, Warren Burger has stirred more than usual interest. There has been much speculation about his influence and whether he would turn the Court in a new direction.

On many occasions, Chief Justice Burger has demonstrated that he is intensely interested in reform of the judicial process and in prison management. He has criticized the courts for being slow, inefficient, expensive, and unnecessarily cumbersome in administering the law. In 1969, he told an audience at Ripon College, "Our system of trials to determine guilt is the most complicated, the most refined, and perhaps the most expensive in the world" (see *New York Bar Journal,* October 1969, page 451). In November 1970, he argued before a Pennsylvania audience for the elimination of jury trials in most civil cases. On Christmas Day, 1970, he wrote a memorandum to all Federal judges urging more efficient handling of cases: "Public patience is running out and we must respond." In a speech before the New York City bar, February 17, 1970, he emphasized the inadequacy of the prison system. The word is out in Washington that the chief justice is an active lobbyist for judicial reform.

[1] Text of the speech delivered August 10, 1970. Published by permission.
[2] For biographical note, see Appendix.

On August 10, 1970, the chief justice delivered his first "State of the Federal Judiciary Address" to the opening assembly of 2,500 delegates of the American Bar Association convention meeting at Powell Symphony Hall, St. Louis, Missouri. The speech was carried to the entire nation via the three networks on prime time. The address, reported to have gone through six drafts, was twenty-five minutes long and was interrupted by applause three times. The response was enthusiastic; there were fifteen hundred letters and over three hundred editorials. Aside from the President's messages, Burger's address was perhaps the most widely circulated speech of the year. The chief justice has implied that he may follow the precedent of the President's State of the Union speeches and report annually on his observations.

Newsweek (August 24, 1970) observed that "his tone at moments was less chief justice than chairman of the board." It is true that the speech is full of facts but is provocative—if not eloquent. Roscoe and Geoffrey Drummond said, "His voice needs to be heard —and heeded." Throughout the year, he continued to discuss court reform.

His proposition was that speedier trials would be a deterrent to crime. He suggested reforming the courts to enable them to try criminals within sixty days of indictment. The speech falls into a problem (slow justice)—solution (appoint court administrators) organization. He sought to enlist the help of lawyers in implementing reform, and he urged cooperation between Federal and state courts.

The Burger point of view was given support by President Nixon when he spoke to several hundred lawyers and judges attending the National Conference on the Judiciary at Williamsburg, Virginia, March 11, 1971. He cited the Burger speech and advocated similar reforms.

When President Segal and the Board of Governors of this Association invited me to discuss the problems of the Federal courts with you, as leaders of the legal profession, my mind turned at once to one of the great statements on the problems of the administration of justice. That was Dean Roscoe Pound's famous speech to this Association at its meeting sixty-four years ago this summer. He said then that the work of the courts in the twentieth century could not be carried on with the methods and machinery of the nineteenth century.

If you will read Pound's speech, you will see at once that
we did not heed his warning, and today, in the final third of
this century, we are still trying to operate the courts with
fundamentally the same basic methods, the same procedures
and the same machinery he said were not good enough in
1906. In the supermarket age we are trying to operate the
courts with cracker-barrel corner-grocer methods and equipment—vintage 1900.

I would not be warranted in coming here today if I spent
our very limited time reminding you what is good about our
courts, or about the splendid and dedicated judges and
others, most of whom are overworked to make the system
function. I wish the public could know what the Association
has accomplished first in the support of public defender programs and now more recently in providing free legal services
for people long unrepresented in civil matters. My responsibility today, however, is to say to you frankly—even bluntly—
what I think is wrong with our judicial machinery and what
can and must be done to correct it in order to make the system of justice fulfill its high purpose.

The changes and improvements we need are long over-
due. They will call for a very great effort and they may cost
money; but if there are to be higher costs they will still be a
small fraction, for example, of the $200 million cost of the
C-5A airplane since the entire cost of the Federal judicial
system is $128 million annually. Military aircraft are obvi-
ously essential in this uncertain world, but surely adequate
support for the Judicial Branch is also important.

Wall Street experts recently estimated that American citizens and businesses spend more than $2 billion a year on pri-
vate security and crime control. Aside from the ominous implications of such private policing in a free society, just think
what $2 billion could do for public programs to prevent
crime and enforce law. That is where such support belongs.

More money and more judges alone is not the primary
solution. Some of what is wrong is due to the failure to apply

the techniques of modern business to the administration or management of the purely mechanical operation of the courts—of modern record keeping and systems planning for handling the movement of cases. Some is also due to antiquated, rigid procedures which not only permit delay but often encourage it.

I am confident that if additional costs arise in the process of making needed changes and improvements in the management of the judicial system, Congress will support the courts. But judges must demonstrate the needs clearly. Congress is harassed with demands for more appropriations for more and more new programs, each of which is labeled a high priority. We must first show Congress and the public that we are making the best possible use of what we already have and it is here that improved methods and skilled management techniques will count. These additions of equipment and personnel will cost relatively little in relation to the whole budget.

You know that in this brief report I can do no more than touch highlights and more detailed treatment of these problems must follow. I hope we can provoke debate—even controversy—to explore and test what I have to say. With increasing urgency every one of my distinguished predecessors from Chief Justices Taft and Hughes to Chief Justice Earl Warren have pressed these matters, but today I place this burden squarely on you, the leaders of the legal profession, in common with all judges. If the 144,000 lawyers you represent in 1,700 state and local bar associations will act promptly, you will prevent a grave deterioration in the work of the Federal courts. And you should remember Justice Vanderbilt's warning that these tasks are "not for the shortwinded."

In the Federal courts today the problem areas are essentially in large cities. Here we find in the judicial system no more than a reflection of the complexities created by population growth and the shift to large urban centers. The problems exist where the action is.

In Maine, for example, there is only one Federal district judge and literally not enough for him to do. As a result he has, for fifteen years or more, accepted assignments to go to courts all over the country where help was desperately needed. Many judges in the less busy districts have done the same. It is in the large centers that both civil and criminal cases are unreasonably delayed and it is there that the weaknesses of our judicial machinery show up.

How did this situation come about in the face of numerous additional judgeships added by Congress in the past thirty years?

First, the legal profession—lawyers and judges—did not act on Dean Pound's warnings to bring methods, machinery and personnel up to date.

Second, all the problems he warned about have become far more serious by the increase in population from 76 million in 1900 to 205 million in 1970, and the growth of great cities and increase in the volume of cases.

Third, entirely new kinds of cases have been added because of economic and social changes, new laws passed by Congress and decisions of the courts. All this represents the inevitability of change and progress.

In this twentieth century, wars, social upheaval, and the inventiveness of Man have altered individual lives and society. The automobile, for example, did more than change the courting habits of American youth—it paved the continent with concrete and black top; it created the most mobile society on earth with all its dislocations; it led people from rural areas to crowd the unprepared cities. The same automobile that altered our society also maimed and killed more persons than all our wars combined and brought into the courts thousands of injury and death cases which did not exist in 1900. Today automobile cases are the largest single category of civil cases in the courts.

All this ferment of wars, mobility of people, congestion in the cities, and social changes produced dislocations and unrest that contributed to an enormous increase in the rate of crime. In a free society such as ours these social and economic upheavals tend to wind up on the doorsteps of the courts. Some of this is because of new laws and decisions and some because of a tendency that is unique to America to look to the courts to solve all problems.

From time to time Congress adds more judges but the total judicial organization never quite keeps up with the caseload. Two recent statutes alone added thousands of cases relating to commitment of narcotics addicts and the mentally ill. These additions came when civil rights cases, voting cases and prisoner petitions were expanding by the thousands.

Meanwhile criminal cases, once a stable figure in the Federal courts, were increasing. Added to that the records show that in all Federal district courts the time lapse in criminal cases from indictment to sentence has doubled.

To illustrate some of the changes, consider just a few figures:

From 1940 to 1970:

> Personal injury cases multiplied five times
>
> Petitions from state prisoners seeking Federal habeas corpus relief increased from 89 to over 12,000
>
> During this period Congress increased the number of judges by 70 per cent, while the total number of cases filed in the Federal district courts nearly doubled

But the increase in volume of cases is not by any means the whole story. Experienced district judges note that the actual trial of a criminal case now takes twice as long as it did ten years ago because of the closer scrutiny we now demand as to such things as confessions, identification witnesses, and evidence seized by the police, before depriving any person of his freedom. These changes represent a deliberate commitment on our part—some by judicial decision and some by legislation—to values higher than pure efficiency when we are dealing with human liberty. The impact of all the new factors—and they are many and complex—has been felt in both state and Federal courts.

The Criminal Justice Act of 1964 guaranteed a lawyer for criminal defendants—at public expense for the indigent—and along with it appeals at public expense. The Bail Reform Act of 1966 authorized liberal release before trial without the conventional bail bond. Each of these Acts was an improvement on the existing system, but we can now see what was produced by their interaction in a period when crime was increasing at a startling rate. The impact was most noticeable in Washington, D.C., where Federal courts handle all felony cases. Defendants, whether guilty or innocent, are human; they love freedom and hate punishment. With a lawyer provided to secure release without the need for a conventional bail bond, most defendants, except in capital cases, are released pending trial. We should not be surprised that a defendant on bail exerts a heavy pressure on his court-appointed lawyer to postpone the trial as long as possible so as to remain free. These postponements—and sometimes there are a dozen or more—consume the time of judges and court staffs as well as of lawyers. Cases are calendared and reset time after time while witnesses and jurors spend endless hours just waiting.

If trials were promptly held and swiftly completed, and if appeals were heard without delay, this would be less a problem, and perhaps debates over preventive detention would subside. But these two Acts of Congress came in a period when other forces including decisions of the courts were making trials longer, appeals more frequent and retrials commonplace. We should not be surprised at delay when more and more defendants demand their undoubted constitutional right to trial by jury because we have provided them with lawyers and other needs at public expense; nor should we be surprised that most convicted persons seek a new trial when the appeal costs them nothing and when failure to take the appeal will cost them freedom. Being human a defendant plays out the line which society has cast him. Lawyers are

competitive creatures and the adversary system encourages
contention and often rewards delay; no lawyer wants to be
called upon to defend the client's charge of incompetence for
having failed to exploit all the procedural techniques which
we have deliberately made available. Yet the most experienced defense lawyers know that the defendant's best interests may be served in most cases by disposing of the case on a
guilty plea without trial.

A new category of case was added when it was decided
that claims of state prisoners testing the validity of a state
conviction were to be measured by Federal constitutional
standards. As a result Federal district courts were obliged to
review over 12,000 state prisoner petitions last year, as compared with 89 in 1940.

There is a solution for the large mass of state prisoner
cases in Federal courts—12,000 in the current year. If the
states will develop adequate postconviction procedures for
their own state prisoners, this problem will largely disappear,
and eliminate a major source of tension and irritation in
state-Federal relations.

There is another factor. It is elementary, historically and
statistically, that the system of courts—the number of judges,
prosecutors, and of courtrooms—has been based on the premise that approximately 90 per cent of all defendants will
plead guilty leaving only 10 per cent, more or less, to be tried.
That premise may no longer be a reliable yardstick of our
needs. The consequence of what might seem on its face a
small percentage change in the rate of guilty pleas can be
tremendous. A reduction from 90 per cent to 80 per cent in
guilty pleas requires the assignment of twice the judicial
manpower and facilities—judges, court reporters, bailiffs,
clerks, jurors and courtrooms. A reduction to 70 per cent
trebles this demand.

This was graphically illustrated in Washington, D.C.,
where the guilty plea rate dropped to 65 per cent. As recently
as 1950, three or four judges were able to handle all serious
criminal cases. By 1968, twelve judges out of fifteen in active

service were assigned to the criminal calendar and could barely keep up. Fortunately few other Federal districts experienced such a drastic change, but to have this occur in the national capital, which ought to be a model for the nation and a show place for the world, was little short of disaster.

Changes in the laws that are part of what we call the "revolution in criminal justice," which began as far back as the 1930s, have brought this about. Anyone who questions these changes must recognize that until the past two decades criminal justice was the neglected stepchild of the Law.

There is a widespread public complaint reflected in the news media, in editorials and letters to the editor, that the present system of criminal justice does not deter criminal conduct. That is correct, so far as the crimes which trouble most Americans today. Whatever deterrent effect may have existed in the past has now virtually vanished as to such crimes.

If ever the law is to have genuine deterrent effect on the criminal conduct giving us immediate concern, we must make some drastic changes. The most simple and obvious remedy is to give the courts the manpower and tools—including the prosecutors and defense lawyers—to try criminal cases within sixty days after indictment and let us see what happens. I predict it would sharply reduce the crime rate.

Efficiency must never be the controlling test of criminal justice but the work of the courts can be efficient without jeopardizing basic safeguards. Indeed the delays in trials are often one of the gravest threats to individual rights. Both the accused and the public are entitled to a prompt trial.

The addition of sixty-one new Federal district judgeships by Congress within recent weeks is the result of efforts which began five years ago. Since it takes time to fill these important positions and new judges do not reach peak efficiency at once, their full impact will not be felt for a long time. We see therefore that the additional judges, needed in 1965, were not authorized until 1970. We cannot solve our problems by meeting needs five or more years after they arise. The time to plan for 1975 and 1980 needs is now, and I hope this can be accomplished, not simply by adding more judges, but by the more efficient use of judicial manpower and greater productivity through improved methods, machinery, management and trained administrative personnel.

Meanwhile, not a week passes without speeches in Congress and elsewhere and editorials demanding new laws—to control pollution, for example, and new laws allowing class actions by consumers to protect the public from greedy and unscrupulous producers and sellers. No one can quarrel with the needs, nor can we forget that large numbers of people have been without the protection which only the lawyers and courts can give.

The difficulty lies in our tendency to meet new and legitimate demands with new laws which are passed without adequate consideration of the consequences in terms of caseloads. This is dramatically illustrated in the current budget of the Office of Economic Opportunity. Congress has granted that program $58 million for legal services. That $58 million is a sound commitment to an underprotected segment of our people whose rights have suffered because they could not afford a lawyer. Few things rankle in the human breast like a sense of injustice. Whether the problem is large or small in the abstract it is very large to the person afflicted. We should applaud Congress for taking that step. But cases cannot always be settled by lawyers and the burden thus falls on the courts. This allowance for Office of Equal Opportunity legal services is almost half of what is allowed for the operation of all the courts in the Federal system. Here again we have an example of a sound program developed without adequate planning for its impact on the courts.

What this all adds up to is that for at least fifty years the Federal court system has experienced the combination of steadily increasing burdens while suffering deferred maintenance of the total judicial machinery—and added to that, much of the machinery has long been obsolete. The foresight of Congress in creating the Federal Judicial Center for research and study of court problems two years ago is one of the few bright spots in the past thirty years.

Now we must make a choice of priorities. When we want to dance we must provide the musicians and the public may well be called upon to pay something more for the Federal judicial system to increase its productivity. But neither costs nor the number of judges can be held down if the caseload is steadily enlarged.

To prepare for this report to you, I asked every Federal judge for suggestions. The hundreds of replies reflected a note of frustration and even anguish at the daily management and administrative burdens that drained time and energy from their primary duty to dispose of cases. That was the common denominator and the common complaint. Federal judges are today in somewhat the position of members of Congress a generation ago, before the Reorganization Act which gave adequate staffs to the members and to the important committee work of the Congress.

The business of litigation is highly complex. To assemble all the necessary individuals is not as simple as TV shows depict. It actually involves the very difficult task of bringing together a judge, twenty-five or more prospective jurors, lawyers, witnesses, court reporters, bailiffs and others, at the same place at the same time without lost motion. The absence or tardiness of a single person will delay the entire process and waste untold time. Countless citizens serving as jurors have been irritated with the inefficiencies of the courts because they find themselves watching TV in the Jurors' Lounge rather than hearing cases in court.

The management of busy courts calls for careful planning, and definite systems and organization with supervision by trained administrator-managers. We have at least fifty-eight astronauts capable of flying to the moon, but not that many authentic court administrators available to serve all the courts in the state and Federal systems. The Federal courts need immediately a court executive or administrator for each of the eleven circuits and for every busy Federal

trial court with more than six or seven judges. We need them
to serve as the "traffic managers," in a sense as hospitals have
used administrators for forty years to relieve doctors and
nurses of management duties. We are almost half a century
behind the medical profession in this respect.

In basic principles, it is indeed essential that we maintain
our links with the past and build carefully on those foundations because they are a result of thousands of years of human
experience in the evolution of the law. There is great value
in stability, predictability and continuity. But the procedures
of the law ought to respond more swiftly—as hospitals and
doctors, farmers and food distributors have changed their
methods. Yet the major procedural change of this century
was the development of the Federal Rules of Civil Procedure
a generation ago. Except for those Rules, Thomas Jefferson
of Virginia, Alexander Hamilton of New York and John
Adams of Massachusetts would need only a quick briefing
on modern pleading and the pretrial procedures in order to
step into a Federal court today and do very well indeed. We
see, therefore, that the judicial processes for resolving cases
and controversies have remained essentially static for two
hundred years. This is not necessarily bad, but when courts
are not able to keep up with their work it suggests the need
for a hard new look at our procedures.

If the picture I have been painting seems melancholy, I
must in fairness touch on a few brighter sides—but sadly there
are only a few.

In recent years the ferment stimulated by Roscoe Pound,
Vanderbilt of New Jersey, Parker of North Carolina—to
name only three now gone—has brought on widespread
growth of judicial seminars, institutes and study centers that
have contributed much and we owe a great debt to my col-
league, Justice Tom Clark, who has worked tirelessly on
improvements in both state and Federal courts.

Perhaps one of the most significant developments in a
generation is the creation this year—under the leadership of
this Association along with the American Judicature Society

and the Institute of Judicial Administration—of the Institute for Court Management at the University of Denver. Here for the first time is a place where court administrators can be trained just as hospital administrators have long been trained in schools of business administration.

Sadly even these bright spots emphasize how painfully slow we are to supply what courts need. The price we are now paying and will pay is partly because judges have been too timid and the bar has been too apathetic to make clear to the public and the Congress the needs of the courts. Apathy, more than opposition, has been the enemy, but I believe the days of apathy are past.

As to the future I can do no more than emphasize that the Federal court system is for a limited purpose and lawyers, the Congress and the public must examine carefully each demand they make on that system. People speak glibly of putting all the problems of pollution, of crowded cities, of consumer class actions and others in the Federal courts. Some of these problems are local and we should look more to state courts familiar with local conditions.

Let me list some major steps for the future—steps to begin at once:

1. The friction in relations between state and Federal courts presents serious problems in both the review of state prisoner petitions and other cases. I strongly urge that in each state there be created a State-Federal Judicial Council to maintain continuing communication on all joint problems. Such a body could properly include a member of the highest state court, the chief judges of the large state trial courts and the chief judges of the Federal district courts. In some states such bodies have already been created on an informal basis.

2. State and Federal judges should continue their cooperation with the American Bar Association to establish and maintain standards of conduct of lawyers and judges that will uphold public confidence in the integrity of the system we serve.

3. We should urgently consider a recommendation to Congress to create a Judiciary Council consisting of perhaps six members, one third appointed by each of the three branches of Government, to act as a coordinating body whose function it would be to report to the Congress, the President and the Judicial Conference on a wide range of matters affecting the Judicial Branch. This Council could (a) report to Congress the impact of proposed legislation likely to enlarge Federal jurisdiction; (b) analyze and report to Congress on studies made by the Judicial Conference and the Federal Judicial Center as to increase or decrease in caseloads of particular Federal districts; (c) study existing jurisdiction of Federal courts with special attention to proper allocation of judicial functions as between state and Federal courts; (d) develop and submit to Congress a proposal for creating temporary judgeships to meet urgent needs as they arise. Some state legislatures authorize such appointments based on a formula of population and caseloads in order to adjust promptly to population changes in rapidly developing areas; (e) study whether there is a present need for three-judge district courts and whether there is a present need for Federal courts to try automobile collision cases simply because of the coincidence that one driver, for example, lives in Kansas City, Kansas, and the other in Kansas City, Missouri; (f) continue study and examination of the structure of the Federal circuits that are now based largely on historical accident and are unrelated to the demands of modern judicial administration and management.

4. The entire structure of the administration of bankruptcy and receivership matters should be studied to evaluate whether they could be more efficiently administered in some other way. Pending studies on this problem should be pressed to conclusion.

5. Over the years various statutes and decisions of courts have altered many aspects of criminal procedure. Meanwhile some of the states have experimented with innovations and

have developed new procedures to improve justice. Since Congress is now considering an entirely new Federal criminal code we should soon undertake a comprehensive reexamination of the structure of criminal procedure to establish adequate guidelines reflecting adjustment to the new code, judicial holdings, and the experience of the states.

6. The system of criminal justice must be viewed as a process embracing every phase from crime prevention through the correctional system. We can no longer limit our responsibility to providing defense services for the judicial process, yet continue to be miserly with the needs of correctional institutions and probation and parole services.

7. The whole process of appeals must be reexamined. It is cumbersome and costly and it encourages delay and it takes too long. Some courts, notably the overworked Fifth Circuit, have developed procedures to screen out frivolous appeals. Finality at some point is indispensable to any rational—and workable—judicial system.

8. We made a wise choice in guaranteeing a lawyer in every serious criminal case but we must now make certain that lawyers are adequately trained, and that the representation is on a high professional basis. It is *professional* representation we promise to give—nothing more—and always within accepted standards of conduct. This Association has now provided lawyers with comprehensive and authoritative standards and it is up to the courts and the bar of every state to make sure they are followed.

I have necessarily left some subjects untouched and others undeveloped but I hope I have imparted a sense of urgency on the problems and needs of the courts. I hope also I have made my point that it is not simply a matter of more judges but primarily better management, better methods and trained administrative personnel.

A sense of confidence in the courts is essential to maintain the fabric of ordered liberty for a free people and three things could destroy that confidence and do incalculable damage to society:

That people come to believe that inefficiency and delay will drain even a just judgment of its value;

That people who have long been exploited in the smaller transactions of daily life come to believe that courts cannot vindicate their legal rights from fraud and overreaching;

That people come to believe the Law—in the larger sense—cannot fulfill its primary function to protect them and their families in their homes, at their work, and on the public streets.

I have great confidence in our basic system and its foundations, in the dedicated judges and others in the judicial system, and in the lawyers of America. Continuity with change is the genius of the American system and both are essential to fulfill the promise of equal justice under law.

If we want to maintain these crucial values we must make some changes in our methods, our procedure and our machinery, and I ask your help to make sure this is done.

THE MIDDLE OF THE JOURNEY

THE MIDDLE OF THE JOURNEY [1]

DANIEL PATRICK MOYNIHAN [2]

Daniel Patrick Moynihan offered an evaluation of the Nixon Administration in "the middle of the journey." Having spent two years as presidential adviser, the Harvard professor announced his intention to leave the Administration to return to his academic duties at Harvard. On December 21, 1970, he delivered an eighteen-minute valedictory before two hundred high-ranking officers, including cabinet members, at a private year-end meeting held in the East Room of the White House.

It should be remembered that Nixon's appointment of Moynihan, a liberal who had served under both the Kennedy and Johnson Administrations, came somewhat as a surprise to many observers. It was suggested that he was brought into the Administration to satisfy the liberal wing of the party. Melvin Maddocks described Moynihan as "a witty valuable man, nicknamed the White House leprechaun by journalists who cherished him for his quotability" (*Christian Science Monitor,* April 20, 1971). During his tenure he had not been at all timid about scolding some of the President's associates. He had had significant influence on the President with reference to the Family Assistance Plan, which embraced a form of guaranteed minimum income.

The speech was carefully prepared; in fact, in delivering it he read his remarks from manuscript. In order to make sure that he was reported correctly, he made a tape available for newsmen. Robert B. Semple, Jr., of the New York *Times* described the speaker as "the tall, elegantly dressed but inescapably rumpled Mr. Moynihan. . . . At once witty and somber, his remarks combined a tough realism about the monumental tasks facing American Government with more than a trace of Irish romanticism about what the Nixon Administration had thus far done about these problems." Receiving the speech with enthusiasm, his peers gave him a standing ovation when he finished. In response, the President said, "Every time we get a little down, every time we need a little inspiration, we're going to want to call him back to give it to us." The

---

[1] Address delivered December 21, 1970, East Room, The White House, Washington, D.C. Quoted by permission.

[2] For biographical note, see Appendix.

Wall Street Journal thought enough of the speech to publish it in full on the editorial page—it was, in fact, one of the few speeches of the year to receive such treatment from that newspaper.

Moynihan has an engaging style. His speech reflects his academic training, his wide reading, and his sensitivity to language; but, at the same time, it is clothed in simple direct diction which at times has a poetic flavor. The speech is among the best of the year. It is refreshing to encounter a positive statement about the President and his program.

Mr. President, Mr. Vice President, members of the Cabinet:

I feel, sir, not unlike a character in one of the Disraeli novels of whom it was said he was a man distinguished for ignorance, as he had but one idea, and that was wrong. It was my presumption that after Secretary Rogers and Dr. Shultz had spoken that there might be still something of very great import that I might say.

If that is not the case, I think it may be just as interesting to find how very consummate are the things which the three of us have chosen to say on this occasion, suggesting that there is some reality to which we are responding.

As the President has said, we are now in the middle of the journey. Where it will end we do not know. It is no longer even clear where it began, our senses having long since been dulled by the relentless excess of stimulus which is the lot of any who involve themselves in American Government.

It may be of some use, then, to try to reconstruct the circumstances in which the President was elected, and formed his Administration, just two years ago.

It seemed the worst of times. It was the habit then to speak of the nation as divided, and to assert that the situation was grave beyond anything since the Civil War itself. This was misleading. The country was not so much divided as fragmented; it was coming apart. The war in Asia, undeclared and unwanted, misunderstood or not understood at all, pursued by decent men for decent purposes but by means, and with consequences, that could only in the end be heartbreaking, had brought on an agony of the spirit that had had no counterpart in our national experience.

The agony was elemental, irresolvable, and nigh to universal. No matter what one's view of the nation might be, events in Vietnam contradicted that view. Not long before the war in Asia began a French Dominican priest wrote that "Either America is the hope of the world, or it is nothing." An astonishingly large cohort of Americans concluded, in the course of the 1960s, that it was nothing.

The agony of war was compounded by and interacted with the great travail of race which, once again, not so much divided as fractured the society. Racial bondage and oppression had been the one huge wrong of American history, and when at last the nation moved to right that wrong the damage that had been done proved greater than anyone had grasped.

An ominous new racial division made its appearance, and with it also a new sectional division, unattended and underappreciated, but not less threatening.

The economic vitality of the nation was imperiled. The war disrupted the economy and then dictated that the onset of peace would do so as well.

In such circumstances confidence in American Government eroded. Government was not to be believed, nor was much to be expected of it. Save fear. Government had begun to do utterly unacceptable things, such as sending spies to the party conventions in 1968.

It all comes together in the story of the man who says "They told me if I voted for Goldwater there would be half a million troops in Vietnam within the year. I voted for him, and by God they were right."

How then could it have been otherwise than that the election of 1968 would begin in violence and end in ambiguity? It was clear enough who had won, albeit barely, but not at all certain what had won.

Then came the President's inaugural address with its great theme of reconciliation, and restraint, and—in the face of so much which we comprehend so little—reserve. "Few ideas are correct ones," wrote Disraeli, "and what are correct no one can ascertain; but with words we govern men."

Those words of January 20, 1969, were and remain the most commanding call to governance that the nation has heard in the long travail that is not yet ended.

How, by that standard, would one measure the two years now past? Not, I think, unkindly. To the contrary, the achievement has been considerable, even remarkable.

In foreign affairs the nation has asserted the limits of its power and its purpose. We have begun to dismantle the elaborate construct of myth and reality associated with the Cold War. The war in Asia has receded, the prospect of arms limitation has gradually impressed itself on our consciousness, the possibility of containing the endless ethnic, racial, and religious conflicts that may now become the major threat to world order has become more believable as here and there things have got better, not worse. The prospect of a generation of peace has convincingly emerged.

In domestic matters events have been similarly reassuring. Far from seeking a restoration of outmoded principles and practices with respect to issues of social justice and social order, the President, on taking office, moved swiftly to endorse the profoundly important but fundamentally unfulfilled commitments, especially to the poor and oppressed, which the nation had made in the 1960s.

He then moved on to new commitments to groups and to purposes that had been too much ignored during that period, and beyond that to offer a critique of government the like of which has not been heard in Washington since Woodrow Wilson.

In one message after another to the Congress, the fundaments of governmental reform were set forth. More was required of government, the President said, than simply to make promises. It had to fulfill them. It was on this bedrock of reality that trust in government must rest. The restoration of trust would depend on this.

Since that time, mass urban violence has all but disappeared. Civil disobedience and protest have receded. Racial rhetoric has calmed. The great symbol of racial subjugation, the dual school system of the South, virtually intact two years ago, has quietly and finally been dismantled.

All in all, a record of some good fortune and much genuine achievement.

And yet how little the Administration seems to be credited with what it has achieved. To the contrary, it is as if the disquiet and distrust in the nation as a whole has been eased by being focused on the Government in Washington. One thinks of President Kennedy's summation: life is not fair. But there is something more at work than the mere perversity of things.

In a curious, persistent way our problem as a nation arises from a surplus of moral energy. Few peoples have displayed so intense a determination to define the most mundane affairs in terms of the most exalted principles, to see in any difficulty an ethical failing, to deem any success a form of temptation, and as if to ensure the perpetuation of the impulse, to take a painful pleasure in it all.

Our great weakness is the habit of reducing the most complex issues to the most simplistic moralisms. About Communism. About Capitalism. About Crime. About Corruption. About Likker. About Pot. About Race Horses. About the SST. Name it.

This is hardly a new condition. Tocqueville noted it a century and a half ago. "No men are fonder of their own condition. Life would have no relish for them if they were delivered from the anxieties which harass them, and they show more attachment to their cares than aristocratic nations to their pleasures."

But in the interval this old disposition has had new consequences. What was once primarily a disdain for government has developed into a genuine distrust. It has made it difficult for Americans to think honestly and to some purpose about themselves and their problems. Moralism drives out thought.

The result has been a set of myths and countermyths about ourselves and the world that create expectations which cannot be satisfied, and which lead to a rhetoric of crisis and conflict that constantly, in effect, declares the government in power disqualified for the serious tasks at hand.

The style which the British call "muddling through" is not for us. It concedes too much to the probity of those who are trying to cope, and the probable intransigency of the problems they are trying to cope with. In any event, in so intensely private a society it is hard to get attention to one's own concern save through a rhetoric of crisis.

As a result, we have acquired bad habits of speech and worse patterns of behavior, lurching from crisis to crisis with the attention span of a five-year-old. We have never learned to be sufficiently thoughtful about the tasks of running a complex society.

The political process reinforces, and to a degree rewards, the moralistic style. Elections are rarely our finest hours. This is when we tend to be most hysterical, most abusive, least thoughtful about problems, and least respectful of complexity.

Of late these qualities have begun to tell on the institution of the presidency itself. A very little time is allowed the President during which he can speak for all the nation, and address himself to realities in terms of the possible. Too soon the struggle recommences.

This has now happened for us. We might have had a bit more time, but no matter. The issue is now henceforth to conduct ourselves.

As I am now leaving, it may seem to come with little grace to prescribe for those who must stand and fight. I would plead only that I have been sparing of such counsel in the past. Therefore, three exhortations, and the rest will be silence.

The first is to be of good cheer and good conscience. Depressing, even frightening things are being said about the Administration. They are not true. This has been a company of honorable and able men, led by a President of singular courage and compassion in the face of a sometimes awful knowledge of the problems and the probabilities that confront him.

The second thing is to resist the temptation to respond in kind to the untruths and half truths that begin to fill the air. A century ago the Swiss historian Jacob Burckhardt foresaw that ours would be the age of "the great simplifiers," and that the essence of tyranny was the denial of complexity. He was right. This is the single great temptation of the time. It is the great corruptor, and must be resisted with purpose and with energy.

What we need are great complexifiers, men who will not only seek to understand what it is they are about, but who will also dare to share that understanding with those for whom they act.

And, lastly, I would propose that if either of the foregoing is to be possible, it is necessary for members of the Administration, the men in this room, to be far more attentive to what it is the President has said, and proposed. Time and again, the President has said things of startling insight, taken positions of great political courage and intellectual daring, only to be greeted with silence or incomprehension.

The prime consequence of all this is that the people in the nation who take these matters seriously have never been required to take us seriously. It was hardly in their interest to do so. Time and again the President would put forth an oftentimes devastating critique precisely of their performance. But his initial thrusts were rarely followed up with a sustained, reasoned, reliable second and third order of advocacy.

Deliberately or no, the impression was allowed to arise with respect to the widest range of presidential initiatives

that the President wasn't really behind them. It was a devastating critique.

The thrust of the President's program was turned against
—him! For how else to interpret an attempt to deal with such
serious matters in so innovative a way, if in fact the effort was
not serious?

It comes to this. The presidency requires much of those
who will serve it, and first of all it requires comprehension.
A large vision of America has been put forth. It can only be
furthered by men who share it.

It is not enough to know one subject, one department.
The President's men must know them all, must understand
how one thing relates to another, must find in the words the
spirit that animates them, must divine in the blade of grass
the whole of life that is indeed contained there, for so much
is at issue.

I am one of those who believe that America is the hope of
the world, and that for that time given him the President is
the hope of America. Serve him well. Pray for his success.
Understand how much depends on you. Try to understand
what he has given of himself.

This is something those of us who have worked in this
building with him know in a way that perhaps only that
experience can teach. To have seen him late into the night
and through the night and into the morning, struggling with
the most awful complexities, the most demanding and irresolvable conflicts, doing so because he cared, trying to comprehend what is right, and trying to make other men see it,
above all, caring, working, hoping for this country that he
has made greater already and which he will make greater
still.

Serve him well. Pray for his success. Understand how
much depends on you.

And now, good-bye, it really has been good to know you.

REMARKS AT THE WHITE HOUSE CONFERENCE ON CHILDREN [3]

RICHARD M. NIXON [4]

No living American is so well known as President Richard M. Nixon. Since 1946, he has constantly been in public view. He is remembered as the anti-Communist fighter, the two-term Vice President under Eisenhower, the man defeated in 1960 by John F. Kennedy by a meager 118,500 votes, the defeated California gubernatorial candidate of 1962 who won the presidency in 1968 with about 43 per cent of the votes. And yet, this most traveled man remains an enigma to colleagues, opponents, representatives of the mass media, and to the public. What manner of man is he? Is he on the high road or the low road? Is he conservative or liberal? A ruthless politician? The hard-driving strategist who directs the attacks of Vice President Agnew? The studious introvert who really prefers the quiet of his study to the hurly-burly of the forum? Or is he a compassionate human being who is caught in a maze of impossible decisions?

During the last year all these views have been advanced. Probably no single label has the dimension to encompass the breadth of the personality and influence of an American President. Richard M. Nixon has continued to fascinate writers—particularly journalists.

How can the selection of one or even two speeches give a fair indication of a man so influential in national and world opinion, so prominently before the public, and so aware of the potentials of the mass media? In recent months the President was perhaps most proud of his State of the Union message of January 20, 1971, described by James Reston of the New York *Times,* who is often critical of the President, as "generous, idealistic, and optimistic." It contained a broad blueprint for the future.

The editor has chosen to pass by the more widely publicized efforts and to include here the keynote address that President Nixon delivered December 13, 1970, to the four thousand delegates who came to the White House Conference on Children, a meeting held each decade since 1909. Those attending had been selected on

[3] Address delivered at the White House Conference on Children, Washington, D.C., December 13, 1970. Quoted by permission.

[4] For biographical note, see Appendix.

the strength of their leadership positions in children's affairs. Some tensions that surfaced later existed among the dissident black, Spanish-speaking, and women's groups who were critical of how the administrative officials had structured the conference.

Observers found this speech a considerable contrast to the President's campaign speaking of the month before. It was planned to refute the impression that the "public Nixon" is a "hard-working square who does his best, but cannot touch the soul of people."

The speech is loosely structured and contains much material referring directly to the President's personal experiences: his violin playing, his daughter's reactions, his memories of the Depression, the death of his brother, his chairmanship of the Boys' Clubs of America. The opening and closing paragraphs, although they contribute little to the main theme, do heighten the congenial mood of the speech.

Mr. Secretary, Mr. Mayor, Mr. Chairman, and ladies and gentlemen, all of the delegates to this Conference:

Before I begin my prepared text, I would like to express my deep appreciation to all of you who have come to this Conference, and also for the very special entrance that was arranged on this occasion.

One of the great privileges for the President of the United States, of course, is to hear Hail to the Chief. I have heard it many times since I became President almost two years ago. I have never heard it played better than by the East Atlanta School from over here, an elementary school.

Speaking as one who played a very poor second violin in a high school orchestra, I appreciate all of the work and the talent that is represented therein by the leader who was able to develop those talents.

I am very proud tonight to share with six of my predecessors, starting with Theodore Roosevelt and most recently, Dwight Eisenhower, the honor of convening a White House Conference on Children. I take very special pleasure in welcoming all of you here.

Our concern at this Conference is with the well-being of 55 million individual human beings who happen to be children under the age of fourteen, and who represent one fourth of all the people in America.

When I refer to them as 55 million individual human beings, I mean to put the emphasis precisely on that—on the fact that nothing is so intensely personal as the private world of the child; nothing so removed from the statistical abstractions of a chart or a computer.

In talking about our children, we are talking about our world and about its future, but in the most special, the most human, the most individual sense of anything we do or consider.

The refreshing little flower emblem that has been used as the symbol of this Conference is a reminder to us of one very simple and very basic truth: that the world of the child is different and very special, and full of promise and very much alive.

It also reminds us that whether we speak of a community of 200 people or of 200 million, the important thing to remember is that no two are alike.

I am sure some of you have heard the little television commercial, a musical one, that has the little ditty that goes "No one else in the whole human race is exactly like you."

Because of this, what is right for one child may be all wrong for another.

Here in Washington, in Government, we have a tendency to think about things in the mass, about cities of more than a million or less than a million, of people over sixty-five or those under twenty-one, about whole school systems or health delivery systems.

Just yesterday, I spent a great part of the day working on next year's Federal budget, on billions for this and billions for that, and how perhaps $100 million could be saved here in order to do something we want to do someplace else; trying to balance the needs and hopes of dozens of Government departments and agencies that operate thousands of programs involving millions of people. Sometimes, after a day like that, I find myself reflecting on both the necessity and then the impersonality of it all. Budgets have to be made and they have to be followed because that is the way the real world operates. And governments have to deal with great masses of people because this is the way governments operate.

But how far removed this can get us from the perspective of the individual person. How great a tendency there is in government to lose track of people as people, to get so wrapped up in charts and projections and columns of numbers that we lose sight of what ultimately it is all about.

If there is one thought more than any other that I would like to leave with you, all of the four thousand delegates to this Conference, it is this: to remember that what matters is one person, one child, unlike any other, with his own hopes and his own dreams and his own fears, who lives at the center of his own separate and very personal world.

I am sure that each one of you is here taking part in this great Conference because you do care not only about children in the mass, but about the child. I hope you will help us in government to keep the focus on that one child.

One of the special glories of America is that we are a nation of individuals and individualists. We produce people, not automatons. We recognize diversity not as an evil but as a virtue. We turn not to one institution alone but to many to perform the great task of achieving a better life for all of us.

We recognize, of course, the role for government, for the church, the home, the school, the volunteer agencies that are so distinctive a feature of American life. And we do know that this is a case in which individual cooks, and additional cooks, do enrich the broth.

There is, of course, a large and vital role government must play in insuring the best possible opportunities for the child.

Tonight I would like to speak briefly to you about just one government program, a Federal Government program presently being considered by the United States Senate, which I believe particularly deserves your support.

The great issue concerning family and child welfare in the United States is the issue of family income.

For generations, social thinkers have argued that there is such a thing as a minimum necessary family income, and that no family should be required to subsist on less. It is a simple idea, but very profound in its consequences.

On August 11, 1969, over a year ago, I proposed that for the first time in America's history we in this great, rich country establish a floor under the income of every American family with children. It has, in turn, been called by others the most important piece of domestic legislation to be introduced in Congress in two generations.

In terms of its consequences for children, I think it can be fairly said to be the most important piece of social legislation in the history of this nation. I am sure you know the story of the legislation. In April, it passed the House of Representatives by almost 2 to 1. Then it became mired down in the Senate. It is still stuck there, but it is not lost. There is still an opportunity for the Ninety-first Congress to change the world of American children by enacting Family Assistance.

In these closing days of that Congress, I want to emphasize once again unequivocally my personal support for welfare reform this year, and to urge your support for welfare reform this year.

In the last ten years alone—listen to this—the number of children on welfare in America has tripled to more than six million. Think of it—six million children—six million children caught up in an unfair and tragic system that rewards people for not working instead of providing incentives for self-support and independence; that drives families apart, instead of bringing them together; that brings welfare snoopers into their homes, that robs them of pride and destroys dignity. I believe we should change that.

The welfare system has become a consuming, monstrous, inhuman outrage against the community, against the family, against the individual, and most of all against the very children who are our concern, your concern, in this great Conference, the children it is meant to help.

We have taken long strides—not enough, but long strides—toward ending racial segregation in America. But welfare segregation can be almost as insidious.

Think what it means to a sensitive child.

Let me give you one example. My daughter Tricia does tutoring at an inner-city school here in Washington. She tells me of her deep concern each day to see the welfare children herded into an auditorium for a free lunch, while the others bring their lunches and eat in the classroom.

We have to find ways of ending this sort of separation. The point is not the quality of the lunch. As a matter of fact, she tells me that the free lunch is probably nutritionally better than the ones the others bring from home.

The point is the stigmatizing by separation of the welfare children as welfare children.

I remember back in the depression years—and if this dates me, if you can remember, you can remember, too—of the 1930s, how deeply I felt about the plight of those people my own age who used to come into my father's store when they couldn't pay the bill, because their fathers were out of work, and how this seemed to separate them from others in our school.

None of us had any money in those days, but those in families where there were no jobs and there was nothing but the little that relief then offered suffered from more than simply going without. What they suffered was a hurt to their pride that many carried with them for the rest of their lives.

I also remember my older brother. He had tuberculosis for five years. The hospital and doctor bills were more than we could afford .

In the five years before he died, my mother never bought a new dress. We were poor by today's standards, and I suppose we were poor even by depression standards.

But the wonder of it was that we didn't know it. Somehow my mother and father, with their love, their pride, their courage and self-sacrifices were able to create a spirit of self-respect in our family so that we had no sense of being inferior to others who had more.

Today's welfare child is not so fortunate. His family may have enough to get by on and, as a matter of fact, they may have even more in a material sense than many of us had in those depression years. But no matter how much pride and courage his parents have, he knows they are poor and he can feel that soul-stifling patronizing attitude that follows the dole.

Perhaps he watches while a caseworker—a caseworker who himself is trapped in a system that wastes on policing talents that could be used for helping—watches while this caseworker is forced by the system to poke around in the child's apartment, checking on how the money is spent, or whether his mother might be hiding his father in the closet.

This sort of indignity is hard enough on the mother. It is enough of a blow to her pride and to her self-respect. But think of what it must mean to a sensitive child.

We have a chance now to give that child a chance—a chance to grow up without having his schoolmates throw in his face the fact that he is on welfare and without making him feel that he is therefore something less than other children.

Our task is not only to lift people out of poverty but from the standpoint of the child our task is to erase the stigma of welfare, illegitimacy and of hardship, and to restore pride, dignity and self-respect for every child in America.

I don't contend before this sophisticated audience of critics that our Family Assistance Plan is perfect. Secretary Richardson, who has been before the Senate, will be able to answer questions that you may put to him because he has been before a very, very critical body.

But I am only going to suggest this: In this confused, complex and intensely human area no perfect program is possible, and certainly none is possible that will please everybody. But this is a good program, and a program immensely better than what we have now, and vastly important to the future of this country—and especially to the neediest of our children. It is time to get rid of the present welfare program and get a new one, and now is the time to do it.

For the United States Senate to adjourn without enacting this measure would be a tragedy of missed opportunity for America and particularly for the children of America.

I have dwelt at some length on Family Assistance because of its vital and even historic importance and because now is the time for Senate decision.

This represents, as I indicated, one of the things the Federal Government can do to give children a better opportunity.

There are others: our programs for the right to read, our emphasis on the first five years of life through the new Office of Child Development in the Department of HEW, on education reform, on food, nutrition, and in many others where we are trying to meet what I believe is a great responsibility that rests with the Federal Government.

I know in this Conference you will have many new ideas for things we in government, in the Federal Government, might do.

We shall do our best to meet our responsibility in those areas where the Federal Government can best do what needs to be done. But I would also stress that equally and often more important is what states and communities do, and the school, the church, the family, the mass media, the volunteer organizations, each of us as individuals. For the child is not raised by government; the child is raised by his family. His character is shaped by those people he encounters in his daily life.

I think especially of the millions of Americans who give their time, their energy and their heart to volunteer activities working with children. You know them in your communities —thousands, hundreds of thousands all over America.

Before becoming President, I served as National Chairman of the Boys' Clubs of America. I saw from the inside the wonderful work organizations like the Boys' Clubs and others do, and also the spirit and dedication of the people who make them possible. There are churches and service organizations, hundreds, thousands of organizations all across America, helping. They can help more.

And most important, these volunteer organizations can do what government cannot do: they can give heart and inspire hope, and they can address themselves not simply to children as a group but to that one special, precious child.

Before closing tonight, I would like to leave with you a few very personal reflections from the perspective of the office I hold.

A President of the United States always thinks about the legacy that he would like to leave the country from the years he serves in this office. I think often about that in terms of what I can leave for America's children.

I know that the first thing I would like to do for them is to bring peace to America and to the world. And here I speak not just of ending the war, but of ending it in a way that will contribute to a lasting peace, so that theirs, at last, can be what we have not yet had in this century—a generation of peace.

I speak not only of the absence of war, but also of a peace in which we can have an open world in which all the peoples of the world will have a chance to know one another, to communicate with one another, to respect one another.

The second thing that as President I would like to leave for America's children is a strong, productive and creative economy—one that can provide every family with a floor under its income higher than what is now the ceiling for most of the world's peoples.

I want to leave them an economy that provides jobs for all with equal and full opportunity, jobs producing not for war but producing for peace.

And beyond this, I want, as you want, America's children in the last generation of this century to have the best education, the best health, the best housing that any children have had anywhere, anytime.

I want them to enjoy clean air, clean water, the open spaces, to restore the heritage of nature that is rightfully theirs.

Although we will always have differences here in America, because this is a very diverse country, I hope that government can help achieve a better understanding among the generations, the races, the religions, among those with different values and different life styles.

I would like to do all this and do it in the climate of freedom.

I want this generation of children to develop a new sense of patriotism.

Edmund Burr pointed out that patriotism translated literally means love of country. And he went on further to say that for us to love our country, our country must be lovely.

We do love our country—most of us—but we know it has many unlovely features. I want young Americans to learn to love America, not because it is the richest country, or the strongest, or merely because they were born here, but because America is truly a good country and becoming better, because it is truly a lovely country.

I am convinced that in my term as President we made some progress towards these goals that I outlined and I think that we, by the end, will have made more progress. But even if all these goals could be fully achieved, it still would not meet our duty to our children.

No matter what government does for people, no matter what we provide in the way of income, housing or food, we still have not reached the essential element as far as a full and meaningful life is concerned, because what is most important is that every person in this country must be able to feel that he counts.

We have to let 55 million very young Americans, as well as those a little older perhaps, know that what they do matters, that their ideas count, that the country needs their thoughts, their creativity, their contributions.

I recall Dr. Walter Judd once said that he loved his daughter very much, and then when she asked him to help her with her arithmetic, he really could do it much better than she could, the easiest thing for him to do would be simply to do it for her. But because he loved her, he would not do it for her. He helped her learn to do it herself.

While this Conference will and should make recommendations as to what government can do for children, about how we can make life better for them, let us remember that what is most important is to provide the opportunity for each of our children to participate, for each child.

It is not just a matter of what more government is going to do for him, but how his own life is going to be enriched so that he can do something for his fellow man.

A sense of dignity, a sense of identity, of pride, of self-respect—these no government can provide. Government can help to create better conditions. It can help remove obstacles to the child's development. It can mobilize research and provide services. It can offer advice and guidance. But all these only help to make success possible.

The love, understanding, the compassion, the human concern that touch the child and make him what he can become —these are provided by people, people like you.

And the way we shape the character of the next generation we test our own character as people. And the vigor and the realism with which we approach the needs of the next generation, of each and every child in that generation, tests our devotion to humanity and our belief in ourselves.

I am confident we will meet that test. And I am grateful, very grateful, to all of you here for the concern you have shown, the dedication you have demonstrated, in helping us to do so.

Your recommendations at the conclusion of your conference on Friday will receive the most careful consideration by the various agencies to which they will be referred and by the President of the United States, not only because we in this Administration respect your view, but also because we share your concern. We share your concern about our nation's children, our children. We share your concern that our children should receive the best that America can give them.

Now, ladies and gentlemen, having concluded my formal remarks, I would like to give you a very special invitation and explain the nature of it.

When I learned about this Conference, I suggested to your Chairman, Steve Hess, that Mrs. Nixon and I would like to receive all of the delegates to the Conference at the White House. He said, "There are four thousand."

I checked with our staff to see whether that would be possible, and they figured out that based on an experience over the past two years of moving receiving lines as fast as we possibly could, it would take six hours and eighteen minutes to get four thousand people through the lines.

I said we couldn't do that because I thought the people at the end of the line might get tired by the end of six hours and eighteen minutes.

But I do think you should know that tomorrow the Christmas decorations at the White House will be completed. Those who have seen them think they are the most beautiful they have ever seen.

We have various nights blocked out. Monday night is the Congress; Tuesday night is the Congress; Thursday night are the diplomatic children, and so forth.

But Wednesday night belongs to you.

We have arranged for a special tour. Mr. Hess and his staff will arrange the buses and all the other various means of transportation that are needed to get you there.

We have arranged a special tour of the White House to see the Christmas lights and we hope that some members of our family can be there at least part of the time to greet some of you.

Thank you very much. We wish you the very best.

THE GENERATION GAP

FOREIGN POLICY AND THE
GENERATION GAP [1]

Frank Church [2]

The continuing war in Indochina has had an important part in the alienation of youth. None of the idealism that sent men to foreign soil in the earlier wars of the century has been shared by those who are presently drafted and must interrupt their lives to fight for causes that seem to them meaningless, hopeless, and inhuman.

In the 1969-1970 volume of REPRESENTATIVE AMERICAN SPEECHES, Lester Thonssen, the editor, entitled the section dealing with the war "The Continuing Agony." In the last twelve months, little has changed. The Vietnamization of the war and the announced intention to reduce the forces in Asia provided some lessening of tension; but the agony, nevertheless, has gone on. The uncertain status of the prisoners in North Vietnam, the spread of conflict into Cambodia, the revelation of widespread use of drugs among servicemen, low morale among fighting units, the trials resulting from the My Lai incident, the invasion of Laos, and the continuation of the draft have stirred despair and cynicism. More and more people have concluded that the Administration has failed to keep its promises, that our involvement in Vietnam was a disastrous mistake, and even that our foreign policy is immoral.

Growing more bitter and disillusioned are the youth of the nation. The killings at Kent State and at Jackson State and violence elsewhere were symptoms of deeper attitudes. Why did these incidents happen? Why the rebellion among the young? To find answers, President Nixon created a Commission on Campus Unrest under the chairmanship of William O. Scranton, a prominent Republican and former governor of Pennsylvania. But when the Commission submitted its findings, the President found them un-

---

[1] Address delivered as the Thomas C. Hennings, Jr., Memorial Lecture, Washington University, Saint Louis, Missouri, December 3, 1970.

[2] For biographical information, see Appendix.

acceptable. The President thought that the Commission asked for too much—particularly during a campaign—when it stated:

> Only the President has the platform and prestige to urge all Americans at once, to step back from the battlelines into which they are forming. Only the President . . . can effectively calm the rhetoric of both public officials and protestors whose words in the past have too often helped further divide the country.

With alacrity Vice President Agnew denounced the Report as "more pablum for permissivists." The President and Vice President built their 1970 campaign to help Republican conservatives running for Congress around the issue of bringing law and order to the campuses and to the slums. The suggestion that this attack was chosen to divert attention from the war did little to quiet uneasiness among those that the Vice President labeled as "radical-liberals," "the raised-eyebrow cynics," and the "elite." The rumor that the President intentionally risked a near-riot at San Jose to help Senator George Murphy in California added fuel to the fire. It seemed to many that the campaign widened the breach between youth and the Establishment.

Out of this climate, Senator Frank Church drew the substance for his speech delivered at the Thomas C. Hennings, Jr., Memorial Lecture on December 3, 1970, at Graham Chapel, Washington University. An outspoken critic of the war and a coauthor of the Cooper-Church Amendment, the Idaho Democrat presented an extension of what he had told the Senate (see REPRESENTATIVE AMERICAN SPEECHES: 1969-1970, pages 27-46):

> Too much blood has been lost . . . too much patience gone unrewarded . . . while the war continues to poison our whole society. Whether by a negotiated compromise or by a phased, orderly but complete American withdrawal, it is time to put an end to it.

He addressed an audience of nine hundred composed of students, faculty members, and interested persons in the St. Louis area. A highly accomplished speaker, Church established rapport easily with his listeners. They understood his reference when he quoted Job: "How long will ye vex my soul and break me in pieces with words?" His directness and fluency, first acquired as a college debater and orator, made him more attractive. He was on sure ground with his listeners when he argued the causal relation between the continuing war and the generation gap.

You do me high honor in asking me to deliver this Thomas C. Hennings, Jr., Memorial Lecture. Having served

with the senator in the years immediately preceding his
death, I remember well the maladies against which he fought
during the fifties: wiretapping . . . unprincipled attacks upon
the Supreme Court and its justices . . . racism . . . the fili-
buster, that legislative weapon of recalcitrance . . . juvenile
delinquency . . . and many more.

Tom Hennings turned his energies, for the most part,
upon those afflictions which plagued our own body politic.
He did so during an era when our national leadership was
largely preoccupied with external affairs. So his fight was up-
hill all the way. And when he lost, as he often did, the thing
I would have you remember about Tom Hennings is that he
never quit. He never threw up his hands and cried, "The
system must be trashed!"

In this connection, let me recite a personal experience. A
few weeks ago, I went to Pittsburgh to address the student
body of Carnegie-Mellon University. Though I was well re-
ceived, two plainclothesmen accompanied me the entire time
I stayed on the campus, and I was given a police escort back
to the airport. University officials explained—almost non-
chalantly—that this had become "standard procedure."

On returning to the airport that evening, we drove past
the Hilton Hotel in downtown Pittsburgh. Inside, hurling
verbal thunderbolts at the party faithful, was the Vice President of the United States; outside, the hotel was surrounded
by young people shouting obscenities.

As I flew back to Washington in the gathering gloom, I
kept turning over in my mind that memorable passage in
President Nixon's inaugural address, delivered nearly two
years before, from the steps of the nation's capitol.

"In these difficult years," the new President had admon-
ished, "America has suffered from a fever of words; from
inflated rhetoric that promises more than it can deliver; from
angry rhetoric that fans discontents into hatreds; from bom-
bastic rhetoric that postures instead of persuading.

"We cannot learn from one another," Mr. Nixon had
said, "until we stop shouting at one another—until we speak

quietly enough so that our words can be heard as well as our voices."

Today, twenty-two months later, the shouting is louder than ever. We have grown not closer together but farther apart. Angry Americans clash in the streets, schools burn, armories are sacked, courtrooms bombed. Startling numbers of policemen and firemen are shot in the performance of their duty. Fanatic new groupings boast publicly that they are waging "guerrilla warfare" against their fellow Americans. Violence stalks the land.

American campuses are in the midst of a crisis unequaled in the history of the United States, reports the President's Commission on Campus Unrest. This campus crisis, the commission declared, reflects deep divisions in American society and is seen in "violent acts and harsh rhetoric and in the enmity of those Americans who see themselves as occupying opposing camps."

No longer do we face our problems together. Instead we divide into minority blocs and special interest groups; student militants, hard hats and Black Panthers, to name a few. Factionalism is so much in fashion that those who claim no particular label are lumped together in a grouping of their own and touted as the "forgotten Americans."

As the balkanization of our society worsens, rational dialogue across the barriers all but ceases. "Nonnegotiable" demands are leveled in language foul from faces flushed. *Power* is the ubiquitous symbol and catchword: white *power*, black *power*, red *power*, student *power*, flower *power*.

Intolerant slogans depict the ugly mood:

> America, love it (my way) or leave it.
> Off the pigs.
> Tell it to Hanoi.

And on and on and on.

With Job, the time has come for America to implore: "How long will ye vex my soul and break me in pieces with words?"

The America of my boyhood was a poorer land, marked by breadlines, bank failures and industrial strife. Parents worried about keeping meat and potatoes on the table. Yet I grew up amidst friendly neighbors on secure streets. To be sure, people took their politics seriously. Times were hard. But I can't recall anybody who didn't believe his country was the greatest in the world. Failure to stand up for the national anthem was unheard of, and never did I witness disrespect for the flag.

This underlying belief in the American system—call it old-fashioned patriotism if you will—filled our history and literature. "We are acting for all mankind," Thomas Jefferson had proclaimed, and Walt Whitman, poet of a self-confident republic, had written:

> Myself, I sing. A single, separate
> person, and praise the word, "democracy."

Yes, when I was growing up, nearly everyone accepted our union as the wonder and envy of the world. Longfellow had earlier assured us, from his quiet study in Cambridge, that "humanity with all its fears, with all the hopes of future years," hung breathless on our fate.

Few doubted it.

On such readings did my generation imbibe the humane and hopeful spirit of America. Zestfully they informed us that our free land represented a new beginning, a sanctuary of escape from the ancient oppressions of Europe.

Now I realize that some of my sophisticated friends would scoff at these recollections. They would brand them maudlin. They would say that such days of innocence, if ever they existed, are best put behind us. They would claim to be glad the country has grown up at last, and that the "now" generation is mature enough to "tell it like it is," having freed itself from the sentimental nonsense and mythology of the past.

These "sophisticates" may be partly right, but mostly they are wrong. They forget that any society, especially one composed of so many diverse cultures, races and creeds as our own, is mortared together by common sentiment, by a basic belief in the decency of its purposes, the virtue of its shared ideals, and the soundness of its institutions.

When we turn scornful of these fundamentals; when we lose respect for each other and grow defiant of lawful authority; when the accepted standard of conduct sinks to a level no more demanding than "doing your own thing," then the country starts to come unstuck.

That's what is happening to us today.

That's why we're in such deep trouble.

The trouble stems from no physical disability. Our economic system is a cornucopia of goods and services piled high. Adult Americans prize its monumental productivity. Our sights were set, after all, during sparse years of insecurity and depression. Small wonder that material abundance should have become the single-minded goal—and unique achievement—of our generation.

So we tend to diagnose today's trauma in superficial and self-serving ways. We tell ourselves we have given our children too much. They are spoiled. They were raised permissively. It's all Dr. Spock's fault!

But, in moments of reflection, we grudgingly concede that our children do have a point. If they reject the shopping centers as the hallmark of American culture; if they resent the ubiquitous and deceitful advertisements of beer, cigarettes, cosmetics and deodorants that forever assault our eyes and ears; if they object to how we have cheapened our surroundings in an endless clutter of billboards and neon signs; if they want the air pure again, and the water running clean, and the land given a little more loving care, are they really so awfully wrong?

Don't mistake these for signs of sickness. These are the symptoms of persisting national health. A new generation of Americans, knowing that it cannot add to the *quantity* in our lives, seeks rather to improve the *quality*. In this they are right. We should pitch in and help them.

For the generation gap which matters involves no insuperable disagreement over goals, nor does it consist primarily of the different life style adopted by so many young people. Indeed, when it comes to their long-term beliefs, their aspirations for their country, or their concept of ultimate justice, the views of most young people are less different from those of their parents than is commonly supposed.

The dangerous generation gap, as I see it, has more to do with means than ends. Far too many bright and sensitive college students are "turned off." Whatever word is used for describing their negative mood, whether it be alienated, disaffected, or disillusioned, the fact is that alarming numbers of young Americans are losing faith in the American political process. They believe the system is rigged for war, not peace; they suspect that representative government has lost its vitality, with only the pocketbook interests enjoying representation, not the people. Worst of all, they think that their entreaties, when voiced in the regular manner, go unheeded and unheard.

This pervasive skepticism about our established political order lies at the very heart of the malaise on campus. It makes the cop-out seem respectable; it accounts for the ease with which self-indulgent pursuits can be justified. If nothing can be done anyway, then why not "celebrate" life? Why not make beads, beards and flowing locks the apparel of defiance and dissent? Why not confront the Establishment? If it won't yield, at least it can be discomforted. Why not?

These are the disturbing questions students ask. The malady is most apparent at our foremost universities, where the faculty itself is infected, but it is spreading rapidly through all our institutions of higher learning, undermining confidence still further, encouraging coercion and infusing contempt. If the affliction is to be cured, we must honestly probe for, and eradicate, the underlying causes. Nothing less will suffice.

The charlatans hold that the remedy consists of a simple dose of discipline, a crackdown on campus. It is easy for them to point to any number of disorders which apparently called for sterner measures than those taken. Obviously, no academic institution—or society for that matter—can long tolerate or endure conditions of anarchy. Force unloosed must be met with sufficient counterforce to restore good order. All lawbreakers must be held to account.

Nevertheless, while a gaping wound sometimes requires a compress to contain it, the wound is healed, not by the tape with which it is bound, but by the inner processes of the body. So, if we are to find the deep-rooted causes of our current affliction, we must reexamine our society, review our recent history, and reflect upon our charted course.

A starting place is to recognize that today's typical American parent and disaffected college student see the world abroad very differently. The new generation never perceived in Vietnam the demons their parents envisioned. Unlike our Presidents who overlearned the "lessons" of World War II, most perceptive young Americans never could swallow Ho Chi Minh as Adolf Hitler in disguise, or believe that our failure to fight for a government we propped up in Saigon would amount to another "Munich." They sensed that Vietnam really had nothing to do with American security, the safety of the United States or the well-being of our people. Inevitably, they came to view the conflict as an unwarranted intervention on our part in a civil war in Vietnam which wasn't our affair.

It does no good to tell these young people that "our will and character are being tested." That we shall not be humiliated or accept our first defeat. They do not believe a mistaken war should be won. They believe it should be stopped. That, for them, is the path of honor.

So it happened that Vietnam, now the longest war in our history, severed the line of communication between our generation of political leaders and the campus leaders of student thought. The two groups move on different plains;

they speak in different tongues. Their paths would never have collided, but passed each other by like ships in the night, except for the war. For we oldsters insisted on drafting the youngsters to fight a war which great numbers of them couldn't approve.

Thus, the disillusionment of so many college students in their country and its institutions has its roots in Vietnam. When the power of the state is used to force young men to fight a war they believe to be unnecessary, at best, and wrongful, at worst (under penalty of imprisonment if they refuse), the seeds of sedition are sown. From these roots, every limb of authority is eventually challenged. Whenever a tree trunk is shaken, all the leaves tremble. Once the legitimacy of the government is rejected on an issue so fundamental as an unacceptable war, every lesser institution of authority is placed in jeopardy. Every sacred principle, every traditional value, every settled policy becomes a target for ridicule and repudiation. Caldrons of anarchy soon begin to boil.

Listen to what the President's Commission on Campus Unrest said about the war. Disaffected students see the war, the commission concluded, "as a symbol of moral crisis in the nation which, in their eyes, deprives even law of its legitimacy. . . . Nothing is more important than the end of the war in Indochina."

The war's fallout has debased, on a far broader front, the confidence of young people in their Government. The credibility of the Government, including the presidency itself, has been grievously impaired. Moreover, an awareness has developed—never known to my generation—that the U.S. Government has forfeited its claim to a morality above that of other governments. The napalming of defenseless Vietnamese villages, the devastation of large areas by free-dropping B-52's, the massacres at My Lai—facts like these prevent young Americans from sharing their elders' coveted belief in the superior morality of their country.

Finally, a recognition is forming that the United States can "lose." All American children learn from their schoolbooks that the United States has never lost a war. But the gargantuan image of brave men, unlimited money and massive modern technology bogged down in a medieval quagmire will not soon be forgotten. Shattered lies the myth of American omnipotence and all other premises on which we built our foreign policy in the years following the Second World War.

I should think that the lessons of Vietnam may have just as much impact on young people's conceptions of American foreign policy in the future as the lessons of the Second World War had upon the conceptions of their parents. Having witnessed the involvement of the United States in both great wars of this century, our contemporary leaders drew the conclusion that since we couldn't withdraw in isolation from the world, we must therefore take charge of it. Thus the United States, at the end of the Second World War, stepped into the vacuum created by the receding European empires. Tommy Atkins was replaced by G.I. Joe; American Marines occupied barracks once filled by the French Foreign Legion. Though we believed our motives to be pure—quite unrelated to the practice of neocolonialism with which we stand charged—the obligations we assumed soon came to exceed those of all the old Western empires combined. The United States, without much forethought, pledged itself to oversee the vast regions once occupied by the bankrupt European nations. Overnight, we became the policeman, banker and judge of most of the world.

In place of the British fleet, the U.S. Navy took up the deep-water patrol. From the Mediterranean to the China Seas, American troops were garrisoned at outposts so far-flung as to dwarf the reach of Imperial Rome. In our zeal as self-anointed protector of half a hundred foreign governments, we retained the draft to summon young Americans to battle in places they had never heard of before, a compulsory duty never imposed on French or British citizens, even at the height of their colonial power.

The obsessive fear which drove us to this extremity—the specter of a monolithic communism engulfing the globe—has long since been shown to be illusory. Communist countries are deeply divided. President Nixon is cheered in Bucharest and greeted with enthusiasm in Belgrade. The red titans, Russia and China, hurl invective at one another and engage in sporadic warfare along contested borders.

While these developments outmoded our old concepts, we kept on adhering to the same engrained habits of thought. We continued to see ourselves as the benevolent sentinel of what we still call the "free world," when in truth it is mainly composed, like the Communist world, of despotic governments that are the very antithesis of all we stand for as a nation.

So it happened that American foreign policy fell out of touch with traditional American ideals. In the name of "pragmatism," we embraced every form of government on our side of the tug-of-war. Their frontiers became ours to defend, for which purpose we stationed more than a million soldiers abroad; their internal stability became ours to promote, for which purpose we dispensed more than $150 billion in foreign aid. To be sure, we told ourselves we were financing development, but we decreed that it must take place within the framework of the existing order. Our principal concern, like that of all presiding imperial powers, became the preservation of the status quo.

This objective cannot be reconciled with our historic conception of ourselves as an exemplary society. Americans who believe in freedom at home will not wed themselves for long to a foreign policy which supports despotism in other lands. When the United States keeps sending arms to the Greek colonels who strangled freedom in democracy's home, when we subsidize the Fascist Franco; when we lavish money on a dictatorship in Brazil which is known to countenance the torture of its own citizens, why in the name of decency are we surprised when idealistic young Americans question our purposes abroad and doubt our words?

The remedy—the only remedy—is to bring America home again, not to a neoisolationism of which I am sometimes accused; not to an abandonment of the United Nations or those alliances, such as NATO, which really contribute to our security; not to a condition of military weakness which might tempt our enemies—but home again to the forgotten truth that the first mission of the Federal Government was never to decide which faction should govern some little country on the fringes of China, but to attend to the genuine needs of the American people!

For too long, our people's problems have gone unattended here at home. For too long, our Presidents have been mesmerized by the quests of Caesar. For too long, our resources have been poured into distant lands, with which we have had no former link or economic interest, no strategic stake or postcolonial responsibility.

The time has come to put right our priorities, before we exhaust ourselves in futile foreign adventures, as other great powers have done before us. At song fests we raise our voices to sing: "This land is our land." Well, it cries out for more attention. American cities rot at their cores, the countryside empties of people, family farms disappear. Smog spreads its noxious mantle, water turns rancid, and the problems of waste disposal grow daily more severe. Race relations worsen, the streets are shamefully unsafe. Crime breeds on addictive drugs. And poverty persists amidst plenty.

This gathering crisis in our own land bears far more importantly on the future of the republic than anything we have now, or have ever had at stake, in Indochina. Attention to these festering problems on the home front, reinforced by an ironclad resolve to solve them, would do more than anything else to enlist the energies, quicken the interest, and restore the allegiance of the doubting young.

Such a new direction requires a radical revision of American foreign policy. Massive intervention in other people's affairs must give way to priority attention for our own. Military adventurism—which has kept this country engaged in marathon warfare for the past thirty years—must be replaced with sufficient self-discipline to restore our armed forces to their legitimate role, the defense of the United States. Above all, the American foreign policy tail must stop wagging the American dog!

That accomplished, we could shift focus back upon those internal problems which so deeply concern young people, such as attaining racial justice, eliminating poverty, improving the quality of life and humanizing our institutions. With credibility, we could then beckon young people back into the mainstream of our political process. Let them vote at eighteen; they know more than we did at twenty-one. Let them help us update our horse-and-buggy politics by abolishing the electoral college, so that the people can directly elect the President. Let them assist in the reform of our unrepresentative convention system, so that the voters can have a larger voice in the selection of candidates. Let them plunge in with fresh ideas about changing our scandalous election laws, to curtail skyrocketing campaign costs and impose realistic spending limits, so that victories at the polls are fairly won, not bought.

That's a start. And when we've made it, even the most cynical young people may begin listening again when we remind them that no society of men will ever be perfect, that every wrong can't be instantly righted, and that the best instrument yet devised for pursuing truth is freedom. But governments that tolerate freedom are rare. They are hard to get, in the first place; and they are hard to keep alive. That task, in a free land like ours, must be assumed by each succeeding generation. Its performance is not the prize of a short sprint, but the hard-earned harvest of an endurance contest.

Out of that understanding, we would come together again. The generation gap wouldn't vanish—and we should be glad for that—but it would no longer tear the country apart. Underlying confidence in the soundness of our institutions would be restored. And our horizons would brighten once more with the promise that American freedom will endure.

THE FUTURE OF THE PAST [3]

HAROLD BLAKE WALKER [4]

On September 20, 1970, Dr. Harold Blake Walker, distinguished minister emeritus of the First Presbyterian Church of Evanston, Illinois, and author of "Living Faith," a column in the Chicago *Tribune,* served as guest preacher at the imposing National Presbyterian Church in Washington, D.C. The membership includes Secretary of State William P. Rogers, Secretary of Agriculture Clifford M. Hardin, Chief Justice Warren E. Burger, Associate Justice William O. Douglas, J. Edgar Hoover, and many senators and representatives and their families. The minister in this pulpit faces not only his regular congregation, but also the transients who attend this church for the short time they are in Washington. The location and the nature of the audience dictate that the minister strive for broader statements of more universal concern than would be the case in a more closed congregation. Few pulpits in the nation are more challenging to the minister.

Like many of his generation, the speaker viewed with alarm the impatience of "today's students" and their demands for immediate and dramatic change. Marches, protests, confrontations, burnings, mob violence, and careless talk about revolution caused him to view these events in the light of past experience. He built his sermon around a theme: "The impossible dream of the good society involves an endless struggle to nourish men and women of character worthy of freedom." To achieve his purpose, he turned to analogy.

Concerning this device Richard M. Weaver in *The Ethics of Rhetoric* (Chicago, Regnery, 1953, page 18) observes that the speaker

> sets about moving the listeners toward [his] position, but there is no way to move them except through the operation of analogy. The analogy proceeds by showing that the position being urged resembles or partakes of something greater and finer. . . . It is by bringing out these resemblances that the good rhetorician leads those who listen in the direction of what is good.

[3] Text of speech delivered September 20, 1970, at the National Presbyterian Church in Washington, D.C. Quoted by permission.

[4] For biographical note, see Appendix.

Dr. Walker draws parallels between events today and Isaiah's protest against the rulers of Judah (Isaiah 1:16-17); the observations of John Calvin; the experience of the Founding Fathers; and, of course, his own youthful experiences in 1924. His development probably gave comfort to the older members of his audience. His charge to the "new generation" is in terms of a high road for all ages, the quest for "an impossible dream." A first reading may suggest to the reader that the message is directed primarily at youth, but a more careful perusal reveals a more universal application.

Wash yourselves, make yourselves clean; remove the evil of your doings from before my eyes; cease to do evil, learn to do good; seek justice, correct oppression.—Isaiah 1:16-17.

When I stood on Connecticut Avenue in Washington the night of May 9 [1970] watching streams of young people flowing by after the peace rally before the White House, my mind slid back to January 1924. I was a college junior then, a delegate to the Student Volunteer Convention in Indianapolis. The theme of the convention was "Christian Students and World Problems." The student mood then was one of idealistic rebellion. The war to end all wars had ended in disillusionment and it was clear that the Treaty of Versailles had sowed the seeds of another war.

The seven thousand of us who met at Indianapolis were resolved to change the world. Our motto, emblazoned on banners around the convention hall, was simple: "The evangelization of the world in this generation." We highly resolved to make our Christian faith effective in the world. We were determined to end racial injustice, to support the growing labor movement, and to put an end to war. We were angry because those Woodrow Wilson called "willful old men" had blocked entrance of the United States into the League of Nations.

When the convention ended we went home intending to make our influence felt in the churches and in society. We soon discovered, however, that nobody was listening to us. Thereafter, we marched in parades in support of Norman

Thomas, the Socialist candidate for President, made speeches against war, and joined the pacifist movement.

The emotional climate and the mood in Washington on May 9 and that of 1924 were the same, and yet different. There were fewer of us, for one thing. Again, we met in faith and hope within the context of the Christian faith; Washington, that May day, seemed more angry and less hopeful. Those who spoke to us, men like Sherwood Eddy, Robert E. Speer and G. Studdert-Kennedy, the poet preacher of England, were eloquently provocative and challenging; those who spoke in Washington were bitter and often obscene. There was, however, one thing my generation and the young of today had in common—a passionate desire for peace and for a just society.

Like those who met to protest in Washington, we thought in 1924 that "The Establishment," we spoke of "the men in power," had made a shambles of the world. Without quite being aware of it, the "now generation" and my generation, inherited one of the most persistent and undiscourageable ideals of the past, namely, the dream of a peaceful and a just society. The anger of those who shouted toward the White House May 9 was more than matched in the eighth century B.C. by the prophet Amos, who denounced the sins of Israel's Establishment in words dripping with vinegar. Isaiah, his anger blazing, uttered his protest against the rulers of Judah in the name of God:

"Wash yourselves; make yourselves clean; remove the evil of your doing from before my eyes; cease to do evil, learn to do good, seek justice, correct oppression."

Plato, dreaming of the good society, fashioned its pattern in *The Republic*; Augustine caught a vision of *The City of God* and called men to create and inhabit it. Indeed, from the beginning of time Utopias have been a human aspiration.

So, to suggest the stirrings of social protest today are altogether new is quite unhistorical. Nevertheless, we are in

a time in which wisdom seems to require a current dateline.
Charlotte Gilman understood the mood when she wrote:

> The little front wave dashed upon the beach,
>   And frothed there, wildly elated.
> I am the tide, said the little front wave.
> And the waves before me are dated.

There is plenty of "front wave froth" around us. It
splashes indiscriminately in all directions, but it is only part
of the ancient tide.

The ideal of a peaceful and a just society flung upon us
from the past is an impossible dream, I suppose, but at the
same time progress toward it depends on those who refuse
to believe that it is impossible. Our own Declaration of Independence was an affirmation of an impossible dream:
"We hold these truths to be self-evident: That all men are
created equal; that they are endowed by their Creator with
certain inalienable rights; that among these are life, liberty
and the pursuit of happiness." There is nothing self-evident
about the rights affirmed or the equality announced in the
great Declaration. They were affirmations of faith and hope,
nothing more nor less. Whatever progress we have made
toward implementing the "inalienable rights" proclaimed
by those who signed the document in Independence Hall
has been made possible by those who refused to believe the
impossibility of their impossible dream.

It is suggestive to notice that when representatives of the
colonies came together to write a Constitution for the new
nation they were at least a little skeptical about the unselfishness and the goodness of human kind. They erected a
system of government with checks and balances to guard
against the usurpation of power. With somewhat the same
suspicion of human nature, Plato doubted the wisdom of
democracy, as he said, democracy gives the individual more
freedom than he can manage.

Those who wrote the Constitution were fearful lest The
Establishment usurp power without check; Plato was sus-
picious of the masses, of what we call "People Power." He

was aware that power in the hands of people is hazardous because too many people are disposed to exercise their freedom destructively. People, whether they represent The Establishment, the revolutionaries or the "silent majority" all are infected by the original sin of self-centeredness and self-interest and as a consequence people are in danger of destroying themselves. Not systems, but people who can't manage their freedom, threaten our era.

Any system known to mankind is liable to corruption by human cussedness, whether it be capitalistic, socialistic, Communist or what not. Wreck the system and you still have people on your hands. "Smash this sorry scheme of things entire," and you still have to build again on people who do not manage their freedom in the interests of the common good. Isaiah put the onus where it belongs: "Wash yourselves; make yourselves clean . . . cease to do evil, learn to do good."

When John Calvin was struggling to create a just and peaceful society, he recognized clearly that the good society rested on men and women of moral competence and spiritual commitment. He was acutely aware that either we discipline our emotions and manage ourselves with integrity and wisdom as disciples of Christ or we will be coerced and disciplined by external authority at the expense of our freedom.

The impossible dream of the good society, therefore, involves an endless struggle to nourish men and women of character worthy of freedom. There are no easy short-cuts on the way; no simple solutions to the complex problems of society. As John Milton wrote in *Paradise Lost*:

> Long is the way and hard,
> That out of hell,
> Leads up to light.

If my generation has failed in the struggle, it is we who are to blame, not the system that has undergirded our common life.

The "now generation" cherishes the impossible dream, even as we did when we were young. I dare say we handed the young of today the dream along with some of the obstacles to it. As one young man said to the Cox Commission investigating the Columbia University disturbances:

Today's students take seriously the ideals taught in schools and churches, and often at home, and then they see a system that denies its ideals in actual life. Racial injustice and war in Vietnam stand out as prime illustrations of our society's deviation from its professed ideals and the slowness with which the system reforms itself. That they seemingly can do so little to correct the wrongs through conventional political discourse tends to produce in the most idealistic and energetic students a strong sense of frustration.

The fact is, however, that the system can be changed by people who care enough to work within its context in season and out of season.

I am sure my grandfather would turn over in his grave if he were to come back to a world of income taxes, Social Security, civil rights, welfare programs, Medicare, Medicaid, the regulation of utilities, stock markets, railroads, airlines and a host of other innovations designed to create a more just and equitable society. People who were ethically and spiritually motivated worked within the system and changed it.

The "now generation" wants things to change immediately, if not sooner. Many of the young are persuaded that time is running out and their future is at stake. Pollution and urban decay, war and social injustice threaten the promise of tomorrow and they want things changed now. It is not difficult to understand their sense of frustration when "the mills of the gods grind slowly," and they are not sure that "they grind exceeding sure" to create a social grain adequate to nourish the future.

In their frustration, the young attack the "system," seemingly unaware that no system, however good it may be, will bring the good society without men and women of character and high courage to undergird it. It is suggestive to notice that the "good man" in the Communist system is the man who is pliable, who can be managed by the managers, by the Establishment, and persuaded to accept the judgments of the party without question. A free society, on the other hand, requires men and women of independent integrity dedicated to Jesus Christ as Lord. The Soviet system requires people who can be managed; a free society needs people who in their loyalty to the highest are capable of their own ethical management.

When we were graduated from the university, the commencement speaker told us, "You are the hope of the world." We believed him, but somehow, either the world did not get the message, or we did not live up to the billing. I hope and pray that the "now generation" will be more worthy than we to be "the hope of the world," with faith, integrity and courage enough to implement the impossible dream they have inherited. "Wash yourselves; make yourselves clean. . . . cease to do evil, learn to do good; correct oppression." We leave to the young the dream, the impossible dream.

What will they do with the dream? That will depend on what they believe. If they think life is only a charade without meaning or purpose, the dream will die with them. If they are persuaded that God is dead, and the ground of their being is nothing but shifting sand, they will have no dependable foundation on which to stand while they struggle. If they have concluded there is nothing in life more ultimate than themselves, their idealism will run off like sweat along the dusty road ahead.

If, on the other hand, they believe that the shadows of individual existence come and go against a background that holds together, they will find meaning in their toil to achieve the impossible dream. If they know in their hearts that their dream is God's dream too, they will know they do not stand alone when they stand against the uncaring crowd.

Happily, along with the dream, the young have inherited a sublime faith wrought in the fires of human experience. The faith the past bequeathed to them affirms that the dignity of man is anchored in the love of God; the freedom of man, in his spiritual worth; and his other concern, in the

Master's affirmation that "inasmuch as you do it unto one of these least . . . you do it unto me." It makes clear that, in spite of disasters, something magnificent is going on here, and the challenge is "to do justice, to love kindness, and walk humbly with your God."

We have been charged with hypocrisy. We plead guilty in the sense that our works have not matched the faith we accepted from the hands of the past. Let it be said, however, that our dream was no less sublime than the dreams of to-day's youth. When we were young we sang, "I ain't gonna learn war no more, no more." We thought we were "climbing Jacob's ladder" and building a better world. But when the chips were down, and we were caught in the struggle for survival in the midst of an agonizing economic depression, we began to look out for ourselves; our other concern faltered.

There was nothing wrong with our inherited faith. It was simply that our private preoccupations dulled its cutting edges. We were left without resolution to cut through the barriers to justice and peace. We retreated into a private piety that betrayed the social passion of the prophets and Jesus. We felt the weight of disillusionment and frustration.

Many of us who have passed the midstream of life understand youth better, perhaps, than they think. We remember the impossible dream that once stirred us, the anger we felt when it ran into roadblocks, our resentment against the men in power. We wonder if today's youth will have what it takes, faith enough for the long haul ahead. Demonstrations, marches and strikes are of short duration, here today, gone tomorrow. They require very little stamina or staying power. I wondered, however, as I stood on Connecticut Avenue May 9: Would the young men and women I saw have what it takes to work through the years at the grass-roots, in precincts, in their own homes, in business offices and in government to effect changes to bring the world closer to the impossible dream?

If we didn't have what it took to keep us faithful to our dream, maybe today's young will be better, wiser and more courageous than we. God grant that may be so. Possibly their own spiritual experience, wrought in the stress of their need for meaning for life will lead them to a new promised land of faith and hope and a new dynamic for creative life and service. But surely it will take new and inspired men and women of high faith to push on toward the impossible dream.

Without faith in God revealed in Jesus Christ as the ground of our being and life, the dream of a just and peaceful society is an illusion; with a steadying faith the impossible dream can be approximated. The future of that ancient dream of the past is in the hands of all of us. "Wash yourselves; make yourselves clean; remove the evil of your doings . . . cease to do evil; learn to do good; seek justice, correct oppression."

THE RIGHTS OF WOMEN

IN THESE PRESENT CRISES [1]

Martha Peterson [2]

The present concern for equality among minority groups has stirred the woman of today to look carefully at her place in American life. Caroline Bird, author of *Born Female,* suggests the extent of these yearnings:

> But the most startling innovation since 1966 has been the appearance of a new kind of woman, more alien to American tradition than the flapper of the 1920s, the man-suited career spinster of the 1930s, or the Rosie who riveted the bombers during World War II. Virtually non-existent in 1966, the new, liberated woman can today be found on every college campus and in every sizable American city. (*AAUW Journal,* November 1970)

Betty Williams, editor of the *Journal* of the American Association of University Women, further interprets the goals of "the new liberated woman":

> The old order—the quiescent past few decades when almost everyone from Senator Ervin to debutantes at their coming out parties knew exactly what woman's role was—is passing. Young women—and not just "radicals"—are questioning the most basic *kinder, küchen,* and *kirche* premises and how they relate to human dignity. Working women are casting a cold eye on unequal pay for equal work, and on the executive dining room full of men. Women in volunteer community service are becoming thin-skinned about always being minute-takers and never chairmen. And men are beginning to understand what's wrong with giving women the condescending smile or the third ear. (*AAUW Journal,* November 1970)

These matters and the frightening events of the school year of 1969-1970 were fresh in the minds of the delegates who assembled

[1] Address was delivered at National Convention of Mortar Board, University of Nebraska, June 17, 1970. Quoted by permission.

[2] For biographical note, see Appendix.

at the National Convention of Mortar Board at the University of
Nebraska, June 17, 1970. Well aware of these moods, Dr. Martha
Peterson, president of Barnard College, delivered the keynote address. In her audience was a highly selected and talented group of
college women. Junior and senior women are tapped for membership in Mortar Board, a national recognition society, solely on the
basis of their leadership and scholastic accomplishments.

As a distinguished woman administrator and a former member
of the society from the University of Kansas, Dr. Peterson brought
to the scene excellent credentials. She established rapport immediately. In tune with student interest in the present, she
quickly established that she was not "a real cornball from the rah-
rah days of Betty Coed and Joe College." She directed attention
to "the new battle for Women's Rights." Some may think that her
solution is not specific enough, but she was consistent with the
Convention theme—"Rock—The Foundation"—and the tradition of
Mortar Board in her emphasis upon rationality and responsibility.

Two techniques in the speech that deserve commendation are
her skillful use of the "bear pole" story and her keeping her theme
"in these present crises" foremost in her development.

Members of Mortar Board:

Being asked to be the keynote speaker for the 1970 National Convention of Mortar Board at the University of
Nebraska, has special meaning for me.

In the first place, I welcome any excuse to return to the
Midwest; New York City is magnificent and exciting; I wish
everyone could have the experience of living there. But this
is Home. Even as a loyal Jayhawker I am pleased to be at
the University of Nebraska. I can, if hard pressed, sing
"There is no place like Nebraska" although natural loyalty
makes me prefer the verse of "I'm a Jayhawk" that ends—

> Talk about the Huskers, those old cornhusking boys
> But I'm the bird that makes them weep and wail.

Secondly this is a Mortar Board Convention and I have
never forgotten being tapped for membership in Mortar
Board. As a member of Torch Chapter I learned the poem
"The Torch"; I think I could improvise my way through
"Thy Ideals" and "We Mortar Board Receive You." At least
Kansas and Wisconsin Mortar Boards did their best to
teach me.

But quickly, very quickly, lest those of you of the Class of '71 think you've got a real cornball from the rah-rah days of Betty Coed and Joe College on your hands, let's move to the present. And what a present it is!

Your theme "Rock—The Foundation" attests to that.

My title "In These Present Crises" confirms it.

If I had any hesitation about this assignment it came from wondering what on earth I could say to individuals like you, strong-minded, able, forceful—of differing ages, political persuasions, heritages—that might stimulate you to more effective action at a time when crises seem to rock the foundations on which our beliefs, thoughts and actions rest.

A number of years ago I went with a friend for a ten-day canoeing and camping trip in the Quetico-Superior Wilderness area on the border between Minnesota and Ontario, Canada. My companion was an experienced camper and a physician; we both could paddle a canoe reasonably well; we were eager to know what it meant to be self-dependent away from the conveniences of modern living. Our outfitter in Ely, Minnesota, assured us that we had adequate supplies for comfortable survival with one warning:

There are bears in the area where you are going; they won't hurt you, but they have learned to like campers' food supplies better than what they can forage for themselves, so keep your food up high out of their reach unless you want an exceedingly restricted diet.

A bear appeared at our camp site on the first day out; we immediately built what is known in that region as a bear pole, hung our food pack on it and went confidently about fishing, exploring islands, resting and the other activities of the seven days we stayed there. It was only when we were en route home and saw a real bear pole at another campsite that we realized how inadequate the bear pole we had built was. It might have deterred a bear the size of a beagle dog, but Quetico-Superior bears could have gotten our food with no great exertion. Our days of wilderness camping had been a success because we had lowered our level of anxiety without adequately coping with a real and present crisis.

Let us consider briefly the nature of crises. They are commonplace in all our lives right now. We live in a time where a discussion of economics, politics, environment, health care, the disillusionment of youth, must always be examined under the rubric "in the present crisis."

There are catastrophes, acts of God if you will, the true accidents—crises in an environment over which we have no immediate control—to which as individuals, communities and nations we rise, first to meet the immediate problem, then to see how such an event can be controlled in the future. Hurricanes, tornadoes, floods, the bombing of Pearl Harbor, the earthquake in Peru, Asian flu, the explosion of the oxygen tank in Apollo 13, the appearance of cancer in a friend or patient, are examples of such crises. These events may change an individual's, a family's, a community's life pattern, but since no one can really be held responsible, since we really cannot turn the clock back, we adjust as best we can and direct our energies toward rebuilding, preventing recurrences, and readjusting. The mentally and physically healthy individual accepts risk as part of life and may even be stimulated to greater productivity by it.

Then there are the crises that are humanly induced without any apparent uncontrollable change in the environment itself. Mass hysteria, individual or group paranoia, are pathological examples of such human-induced crises. Physicians are prepared to treat psychosomatic illnesses; bankers to cope with rumors that might lead to a run on the bank; police to handle crowds reacting to a speech by Jerry Rubin. On the personal level each individual knows there are limits of personal tolerance: the neighbor's TV; the sassy saleslady or the strange discoloration of a spot on one's leg may alarm any one of us. The stranger walking behind us in the street can create within us, no matter the innocence of his intention, a crisis situation influencing his behavior. We cope with these by trying to "cool" the situation, reduce the level of anxiety, create a new, more rewarding kind of activity; we turn to psychiatry, either home style or professional—in order to learn how to continue to meet each day's frustrations. Whether what we do is appropriate may not be as important as how we see what we do. On our camping trip we really didn't cope adequately with the bears in the Quetico-Superior area but we thought we did, and fortunately that was adequate on that occasion.

Not all personally induced crises need to be controlled or subdued for they can produce more positive results. Elizabeth Blackwell, the first woman M.D. in the United States, had a passion to become a physician. Gauguin's was to be a painter, Hillary's to climb Everest. These internal crises created a source of energy to accomplish the impossible; personal crises can lead to public good.

But the crises that face us and discourage us in this summer of 1970 grow out of both the situations over which we have no control and the individual reactions to these situations.

Margaret Mead in her recent book *Culture and Commitment* quotes a fifteen-year-old boy who says "things just aren't right and we must do something about it." That was a reasonable quotation in early spring. Now it seems almost too mild to describe our current state of mind. Our environment has changed so politically, economically, socially, internationally, ecologically, and we are so tightly wrapped up in these changes that we all seem to be saying "things are terribly wrong and we wonder if they can ever be fixed."

It is this kind of world in which each of us here who has been labeled as a woman leader, lives. We are in a time of crisis that cannot be set right by calming fears or learning to accept reality, much as that might be useful to the over-stimulated. It is a crisis that mandates real change in the public process, on the college campus, in our commitments and neighborhoods, in our attitudes toward each other, our capacity to effect change, if we are to cope with the frenzy and depressing pall under which we live.

Your questions and mine relate to our part in the present crisis. To despair or to preach doom is not helpful; it ap-

parently does little good to march about carrying signs proclaiming where we stand on peace or smog or General Mo-
tors, or Bobby Seale. We may have signed a petition for
peace daily since May 1; we may also have begun to wonder
if petitioning cannot be overdone. It's just possible we have
reached a point of diminishing return in issuing the less than
pungent statements of position written by committees. Writing statements and circulating petitions may produce a personal sense of release, and as a first expression can be helpful, but what more is there to do. Should we curtail our
spending to curb inflation; certainly we can stop littering
without much effort; some of us will become involved in
political campaigns and undoubtedly will continue to write,
wire and visit Washington if for no other reason than to
give credence to a statement in the *Times* a few Sundays ago
that indicated that long-time observers of the Washington
scene are beginning to suspect that the nation may be in the
throes of a fundamental political trauma.

Many of us do believe we are in a state of crisis and will
seek means to express our personal convictions as nonvio-
lently as possible. Only somehow or other this is not totally
satisfying; or rewarding. It is what any interested citizen can
and probably should do, no matter what the crisis. Each of
us wants, seeks, a more personal expression of her values,
her concerns, her personal worth.

Let me speak now to the role of the educated woman
leader in the 1970s. In modern rhetoric one of the nonnegotiable demands on you is that you are a woman, educated
and recognized by your peers as a leader, else you would not
be here.

There is a new feminism abroad these days that may
create some crises for you as a woman, and that may also
alter your effectiveness in the other crises. You may wish to
reject this new feminism because its stridency shocks you,
to ignore it because it does not apply to you; you may believe
in the long-range value of personal victories to legal decision; you may believe in the steel hand in a velvet glove,

or you may just prefer velvet. But will you or can you afford such disdain, disengagement or high-minded nobility in regard to woman's role if you are to be as effective a woman and a leader as you have the potential to be.

The new battle for Women's Rights appears in a variety of forms.

Recently the National Conference of Christians and Jews and the Women's Unit from the Governor's Office in New York sponsored a conference in New York City. A resolution was adopted at the conference demanding $100 million from one hundred top advertising firms to support child care, free abortion and legal services for women.

Later in the week a group of women picketed the Playboy Club asking that it be converted into a Day Care Center for Children to repay partially the exploitation of women inspired by the Playboy philosophy. Kate Millett's book on *Sexual Politics* which will appear in July, published by Harper & Row, will further stress the current emphasis of the Women's Liberation group on this exploitation of women because of the biological and cultural consequences of being female and therefore the bearer of children.

Where do you stand on legalized abortion, child care centers, exploitation of women as a sex symbol in advertising? You may not really care about these issues; you may insist that these are crises fabricated in the minds of the members of the Women's Liberation movement. But that does not mean they are not real or worthy of concern.

There are other concerns among the new feminists.

On June 9 the Labor Department issued guidelines designed to eliminate discrimination against women in jobs paid for with Federal funds. The new guidelines prohibit newspaper advertising labeled "male and female" unless sex is "a bona fide" occupational qualification; forbid penalties for women employees for taking time off to bear children and the denial of employment to women with young children "unless the same exclusionary policy" exists for men.

These new guidelines were recommended by a task force of distinguished men and women who reported six months ago to the President on women's rights and responsibilities. This report has just been released by the White House; it indicates that the United States "in its two hundredth anniversary lags behind some newly emerging countries in the role ascribed to women." You should read it even if you really do not believe that you want to work when you are pregnant and don't mind that jobs are labeled "male" or "female." You may say, "Any woman with ability and energy can accomplish whatever she is willing to sacrifice enough to do, and so what is the problem."

But are you sure?

A recent survey by The American Association of University Women of their members and their husbands or male colleagues, produced these findings:

A quarter of the women reported experiencing sex discrimination; the same proportion of men reported seeing discrimination against women.

Eighty-four per cent of the women and 77 per cent of the men felt that job discrimination because of sex existed.

The Women's Bureau reports that the salary of the median woman wage earner in 1968 was 58.2 per cent of that of the median male wage earner. And the gap has been widening; women were better off in 1955 when their median wages were 63.9 per cent that of men's.

And what about college women.

At Columbia University Commencement two weeks ago, the Columbia Women's Liberation distributed a leaflet to parents of Barnard graduates that said:

Congratulations on your daughter's graduation.
But can she Type?

With some restraint the leaflet pointed out that a woman graduate's prospects for employment, for graduate or professional school admission, were different from the man graduate's, usually to the disadvantage of women.

Only 11 per cent of the doctorates in the sixties were women; only 6.7 per cent of the physicians are women; only 35 per cent of the lawyers are women; and only one half of 1 per cent of working women earn over $10,000 a year.

Is there a kind of second-class citizenship for women, professionally and economically after graduation from college? Statistics and studies seem to point to this. Are the differences based on the necessities of being a wife and mother? Or are the crises in some women's lives created by unnecessary restriction on women which we accept unquestionably?

We may decide that the way things are for women is natural or at best should be accepted. Then as women leaders we have a real battle ahead with the new feminists. Or we may decide that this is a crisis of the seventies in which our leadership and ability is sorely needed, and seek to give the solid kind of leadership that is needed. To paraphrase awkwardly "As long as there is discrimination that denies one individual opportunities for which she is qualified, no other responsible individual can refuse to act."

I asked earlier how each of us could prove her personal worth in these overwhelming and sometimes discouraging times. I have suggested one responsibility we cannot ignore—the elimination of discrimination based on sex. Let me suggest another area in which there are crises we cannot ignore.

The volatility on the college campus and the disenchantment of people in general with the academic community is of crisis proportions. There may be less polarization of individuals on campus as they face attack and criticism from outside, but no real progress in achieving the values the academic community represents without the support and respect of alumnae, trustees, politicians, parents and the general public.

The Mortar Board Chapter may decide to enter positively into improving the status of women or the reading level of the third grades in whatever ghetto area is nearby, or in registering voters for the November election, but if they are not trusted, they will talk only to each other. Faculty and students may redouble their efforts to give new life to the liberal arts curriculum, but if the principles of academic freedom and inquiry are seen as synonyms for anarchy and irresponsibility, the efforts will have to go into self-defense rather than creative thought. And those who so desperately wish to be a part of the public process this fall may notice a wariness on the part of politicians lest the new manpower be a kiss of death.

Commonly held views of what colleges and students are like these days may be based on accurate assessment of some campus events. But to dismiss the contributions of colleges and universities as unnecessary, or to assume that only stringent measures of reform should be applied from outside, are self-defeating steps which only increase the crises. The colleges will turn increasingly inward, stifling the all-important exchange with the real world that makes learning relevant; and the world outside the colleges will lose that dynamic and reasoned leadership only education can supply.

Alexander Bickel in a recent issue of *The New Republic* puts it this way:

There is a crisis in this country and it went from bad to worse this spring. But it is not only, it is not even chiefly, the crisis that fashion requires us to shake our heads about. The war has got to stop, the march into Cambodia is a gruesome error, the cities are a mess, our rivers and our air smell awful, and the blacks will not and ought not stand for being forgotten again. But there is another crisis that will incapacitate us from dealing with the ones I have just mentioned. It is not the crisis of allegiance on the part of downtrodden blacks and not the tinderbox of conflict between them and the lower-class whites who confront them, but the crisis of abandonment of reason, of standards, of measure, the loss of balance and judgment by intellectuals and their audiences. The symptoms of this crisis are the incivility and even violence of rhetoric and action that academics and other intellectuals have domesticated into their universe of discourse, and the interdiction of objective discussion of certain problems that they have increasingly tolerated.

This does not minimize the crises in the country but indicates that unless the crisis on the campus can be solved, the other crises won't be. It is this interdependence between campus and community to which I urge you to give your time and efforts.

To begin to find the way through there must be changes on the campus, perhaps first, Mr. Bickel suggests in the same article:

No more vandalism; no more assaultive, vicious speech; no more bullying, simulated or actual. If the reassertion of this minimum of authority should bring strife and violence in the short term, as it may, it will be less strife and less violence than is otherwise in store for us.

Mr. Bickel suggests college and university presidents must achieve this return to sanity. I know, as do all of you, that it will be a joint effort of student leaders, faculty and administration, and when we have found a way we will then be able to bring back the interest and support of others.

A few weeks ago when I was beginning to work on these remarks I came across these notes on a 3 x 5 card: Lowell, Crisis. I decided this had to do with a quotation from a Robert Lowell poem for I had been reading some of his poems in the past year. I could not find anything that seemed related in the books I had so I went to the college library and asked if Lowell had a poem on The Crisis. The librarian said—"of course"—and produced "The Present Crisis" by James Russell Lowell, written in 1844, to support abolition of slavery. You remember it from the verses of the hymn that starts: "Once to every man and nation comes the moment to decide."

I quickly took the book—embarrassed that I had confused Robert Lowell and James Russell Lowell, pleased that the librarian had not caught on to my ignorance. Then I began to wonder about these present crises. Are they so new? Are we living through catastrophes over which we have no control? Or are we becoming sensitized so that we do have the necessary energy to effect change?

Having stumbled onto James Russell Lowell, let me close these remarks with one more line from his poem "The Present Crisis":

They have rights who dare maintain them;

That seems to me to be adequate for our crisis, ladies of Mortar Board.

THE FUTURE OF HIGHER EDUCATION

HIGHER EDUCATION BEGINS THE SEVENTIES [1]

THEODORE M. HESBURGH [2]

In opening the school year of 1970-1971, two university presidents anticipated what was ahead by quoting Charles Dickens' opening statement in *A Tale of Two Cities*: "It was the best of times; it was the worst of times." The violence on the campuses during the previous twelve months and particularly the killings at Kent State and Jackson State could not be forgotten or dismissed. At least thirty state legislatures passed laws on handling campus violence. Chancellor Oswald Tippo of the University of Massachusetts reflected the anxieties of the moment in his opening convocation address of September 16, 1970:

> We will be subject to repressive legislation and serious budget cuts, even warnings of withdrawal of complete state support, if we have any more building takeovers, if we have any more interference with free speech and free movement including attendance at class, if we have continued defacing of buildings and damage to buildings, if we continue to have strikes and other interruptions of academic work, and if we do not keep the campus open for those who come here for the serious purposes of study and teaching.

With the tragic events of the spring still much on his mind, Dean John A. Flower was moved to say at the opening faculty meeting at Kent State University, September 21, 1970:

> We find ourselves as university people in arduous times. . . . Our credibility as honest teachers and seekers of truth has never been so low. We have not yet admitted to ourselves that legions of people external to the university think that professors are privileged far beyond what they deserve to be, that they seem to be inherently lazy, and that they have become not only morally soft, but inciters of discontent.

[1] Address was delivered to faculty of the University of Notre Dame, October 5, 1970. Quoted by permission.

[2] For biographical note, see Appendix.

The speeches of Chancellor Tippo and Dean Flower were only two among many thoughtful and well-conceived addresses made by university and college administrators when they faced students, faculties, and off-campus groups. Moments of crisis usually produce great speaking.

An excellent representative of these academic speeches and a succinct pronouncement of the issues involved is the following speech by the Reverend Theodore M. Hesburgh, president of the University of Notre Dame, delivered to his faculty, October 5, 1970. Expressing well the sentiment of many others, he said, "Good teaching, nay, great teaching may yet be the salvation of the University and of the society in our day."

In the twenty-five years that I have been associated with the university, as faculty member and administrator, I can think of no period more difficult than the present. Never before has the university taken on more tasks, and been asked to undertake many more, while the sources of support, both public and private, both moral and financial, seem to be drying up.

In the 314 years from the founding of Harvard until 1950, we grew in the United States to a total capacity of 3 million students in higher education. From 1950 to 1970, that number and capacity more than doubled to over 7 million students. Maybe our traditional ways of governance have not kept pace with our enlarged size and the new mentalities of both faculty and students. Maybe both we in the universities and the world beyond really expected too much of our university operation. We live in a university world of idea and imagination. But these alone will not insure peace, social justice, an end to racism and poverty.

Maybe our growth was too uneven, with the physical sciences getting the lion's share and all the other disciplines emulating the physical sciences' methodology to qualify for a larger share. This was doomed to failure for, however attractive the humanities and the social sciences are, they become singularly unattractive once quantified, mathematicized, and unattentive to values. Having sold their birthright, in large measure the mess of pottage was not forthcoming.

Maybe our problems relate more deeply than we suspect to the parlous state of the world around us—to its basic malaise, to its anomie, to its frustration and rootlessness. I suspect that we are, in the Western world and even beyond its boundaries, passing through an historical watershed which we little understand and which may be ultimately of more importance than the Renaissance, the Reformation, or the industrial revolution.

I doubt that anyone would be able to label our age, although it might be called the age of frustrated expectations, the age of protest against almost everything, the age of unlimited possibilities and disappointing results. It is an age that can put men on the moon yet create an impossible traffic tangle in every metropolitan center. It is an age of unbelievable wealth and widespread poverty. It is an age of sensitivity to human dignity and human progress in which there is relatively little of either, despite the available resources. It is finally an age where the hopes, the expectations, and the promises of humanity have been more rhetorical than real. Because the university lives largely by rhetoric alone, it has come to be blamed for much of the frustration. In a very real sense, the university has been oversold as the key to all human progress. There is a wide gulf between the blueprint and the reality—the word and the deed.

Given the actual state of the world around us, we in the university are little comprehended in that all of the world's anxieties are focused strongly in the university where there exists an explosive combination of young, searching minds that are invited daily to view all problems and every variety of response to them and a faculty that is problem-oriented and given to play to the generosity and idealism of youth. Also an administration that is only able to survive by responding positively and emphatically to the aspirations and hopes of faculty and students, however impossible they are of immediate accomplishment.

Into this explosive mix comes a strong cry for "law and order" from the so-called silent majority who are not anxious to face new approaches to human equality or social justice if these threaten their hard-earned gains. When the university responds negatively to this demand for law and order, which it rightly construes as "status quo," and continues to insist on stronger priorities for the nation, new initiatives for peace, for equality, for social justice, whatever the shock to the "status quo," then we have a superexplosive situation. The university is judged to be subversive, it is certainly not understood and it loses more and more the public and private support that is needed to sustain it.

It is simply an historic fact that any group, and particularly a university community, does not understand not being understood. What is more serious, young people in the university do not realize how much the university depends upon the support of the larger surrounding society. Even less do they understand that when their frustrations about the problems of the larger community lead them to act in anger and, at times, with violence, there is only one normal response, from that larger community, namely, counterviolence and repressive action. Japanese university students practically closed the principal universities in Japan for a year or so until the Diet passed a law envisioning the permanent closing of some universities, especially Tokyo, the largest. Then suddenly the message was manifest and the violence dropped off.

One might speculate what would happen if some American universities which suffer constant disruption were suddenly closed down for a year or two. It might be healthy and it might be disastrous, but it could happen and it may.

It would have been incomprehensible to mention such a possibility, even speculatively, a decade ago. But it does demonstrate the present state of affairs that it is being mentioned today.

Some have tried to describe the present situation as the politicization of the university. It certainly is true that faculties, even at Harvard and Princeton, have taken rather unanimous positions on the Vietnam War that would have been unthinkable a few years ago. University presidents have also spoken out to an extent that has brought them condemnation from the highest levels of Government and from a broad spectrum of alumni and benefactors. Students who were termed apathetic a few years ago are now deeply involved in political lobbying, electioneering for favored candidates, and protesting the actions of other political figures with whom they disagree.

There is some merit in all of this, but some thoughtful university observers call it the politicization of the university and the end of that objective, other-worldly, balanced and impassionate activity that has long characterized the university. Some see in all of this the end of academic freedom and a call for repressive action.

The fact is that almost every state in the Union has considered in its legislature some punitive legislation against faculty and students—about half of which has been enacted into law. Trustees and governors have practically forced the resignation of a number of presidents, for instance in Texas, Oklahoma, and California. Feeling is running high against many highly visible universities and the witch hunters are out and at work. Both Federal and state programs of support for higher education have been reduced or tied to impossible conditions. Many private universities find themselves hard put to hold fast to the support they now have, much less to augment it. Disaffection with universities, their presidents, their faculties and their students is simply a growing fact of life that will probably get worse.

The great majority of the best university presidents that I have known, respected and worked with over the past years are simply resigning to escape what has become an impossible task: to keep peace inside and outside the university, when trustees cry "law and order" and students condemn this concept as another form of "status quo" in a very imperfect world. Alumni think the whole enterprise is coming apart at the seams, while faculty call for even greater changes than those now taking place. Benefactors lose confidence in the whole unruly endeavor when they are attacked by students or faculty because they are accused of giving money gained through what is proclaimed to be an unholy military-industrial alliance. Parents expect a control over their children which they themselves have never been able to maintain, while the students in turn want absolute freedom and certainly no one acting in the place of their parents, however ineffective these may have been. At this point, the president, who is believed to be in charge although his authority has been monumentally reduced, begins to see that he simply cannot succeed unless the academic community is a real community—something becoming ever more rare in university circles.

Many of the new experimental forms of university governance are aimed at building a stronger university community. Whether or not they will achieve this is simply conjecture at this point. In general, the trustee system has served American universities well, when faculties were allowed to decide academic matters and when students were given a reasonable voice in the arranging of their affairs. One might fault some university boards of trustees by noting that they have generally not represented the broad spectrum of the public they were supposed to represent. There have been all too few women, or blacks, or middle class, or younger people on most boards. Most of them, at least at the great private universities, resembled too much an exclusive club for WASPs (White Anglo-Saxon Protestants). But this is changing as it should, and faculties and students are having an ever larger voice in those decisions that mainly affect them and their lives. Reform of governance alone is certainly not the total answer to the problems that face us.

So far, I have been mainly engaged in an analysis of the present situation facing universities in a changing world. The view, as I have thus far presented it, is admittedly pessimistic. As a committed optimist, I believe that at this time I should attempt to find a few positive aspects of the total picture.

To begin with, student and faculty unrest in our day—a worldwide phenomenon—is in large measure a manifestation of their moral concern for the priorities or the values of present-day society. One would find it difficult to fault them for those things they oppose: war, violence, racism, poverty, pollution, human degradation on a large scale.

It has been a quality and inclination of most young people, since the time that Aristotle accused them of being too vehement about everything, to see the world in absolute terms of good and evil, to be inspired by great idealism, generosity, and enthusiasm, and often to give their all, to man the barricades for causes of justice and equality. Life, problems, and solutions somehow seem simpler to the young who are yet unscarred by the acid of cruel experience. This is not all bad. Maybe the weary and cynical world today, more than ever before, needs this kind of youthful conscience to find its way out of the lassitude and ambiguity that attend so much of modern human life. Maybe the university is the only place on earth where we can bridge the generation gap by common moral concern on the part of young and old, faculty and students. Granting that students are often naive in their concern for instant solutions to very complicated problems, granting their addiction to absolute black and white judgments in matters that are often very gray, granting their lack of a sense of history, their rupture with tradition, and their inability to appreciate experience and competence, they still are concerned and are unafflicted by the anomie that is the cancer of so many of their elders.

Perhaps this calls for a greater dedication to teaching on our part, for great teaching can manifest competence without preaching it, transmit a sense of history without seeming to be antiquarian, show how much patience is to be valued just by being patient with them. Good teaching, nay, great teaching, may yet be the salvation of the university and of society in our day. It has been rather obvious that our professors have in large measure sought distinction through research rather than great teaching, through adherence to their discipline far beyond loyalty to their particular institution. The theory was that research would enrich teaching, but for all too many professors, it has largely replaced teaching. This has not gone unnoticed by the students who flock to the chosen few who still can profess and teach.

I do not believe that the university has by any means come to the end of its road, but I am willing to concede that it faces a fork in the road and must make some real decisions as to where it is going. Generally speaking, I would conclude that the university can and must remain politically neutral as an institution, although its faculty, students, and administrators are free to take their own political stance, indeed must do so when faced with national and international crises with deep moral undertones. It is difficult for a president to do this as an individual, but he must always try to make this clear to the public. I am personally against faculties taking political stances as a particular university body academic, unless the matter is of supreme moral, national or international importance. Students are somewhat freer in all of this because they do not have such permanent attachment to the university. Alumni less so. Avoiding politicization in highly emotional and deeply polarized times is not going to be easy. The threatening loss of academic freedom or academic objectivity is reason enough to keep trying in every way one can.

Balancing the development of research in the physical sciences, the social sciences and the humanities may be somewhat easier now that the golden age for research support in the physical sciences seems to be passing. Since teaching needs all the importance, respect, and reward that we can accord it, giving it some measure of priority may be at the heart of the solution.

The service relationship of the university to the communities that surround it, local, state, national and international, is something that needs great clarification for the survival of the university. In some cases, the university has become too much of a service station expected to solve problems by its actual operation rather than seek solutions theoretically and pilot-test them in a more microcosmic fashion. The university cannot become the Red Cross immediately attending to all manner of social emergencies. It is not an overseas development corporation or a foreign or domestic Peace Corps. It may well have strong intellectual and educational ties to these and other service organizations, but it should never confuse its university identity or task with theirs.

Universities should be ready to experiment with new forms of governance, but I see no great value, in fact great loss, in confusing the specific tasks of trustees, faculty, administrators or students. Maybe we should proclaim more often that the prime function of the faculty is to teach, that of the students to learn and that of the administration to make the conditions for teaching and learning more fruitful. Trustees can be enormously effective to the whole operation if they appoint and protect good officers of the university, help keep the institution financially viable, and support against any power inside or outside the institution the integrity of the whole operation and its best priorities as they emerge from the total community, including the alumni. Every community needs, especially in troubled times, some final authority, some strong protector. Trustees have fulfilled this role for the better universities that have emerged in America.

One is often reminded of Charles Dickens' opening statement in *A Tale of Two Cities*: "It was the best of times; it was the worst of times." I think this can well be said of the state of the university in the rapidly changing world of our day. We can survive the worst if we achieve the better or hopefully, the best.

THE INNOVATION MIRAGE [3]

John A. Howard [4]

Much recently has been said about relevance and about "politicizing" the university. Students argue for a curriculum that concerns the "real needs" and seeks solutions to inner feelings, frustration, and "hangups." The "here and now" must receive primary attention, and the study of the past is regarded as a waste of time. Jon Van Dyke, a visiting Fellow of the Center for the Study of Democratic Institutions, who is twenty-seven, explained these youthful attitudes in these words:

> The young are not burdened with a sense of history. Unlike the old, they are not concerned with whether we are better now than we used to be. Instead, they are only conscious of how bad our society is, compared with what it could be. (*Center Report*, IV, Feb. 1971, page 21)

President John A. Howard of Rockford College considered this line of thought in his opening Convocation Address, September 9, 1970. Committed to the liberal arts, he discussed whether innovation is always "a good thing." Clearly, he declares his position when he says:

> If we permit the thrust for contemporary "relevance" to prevail, then we cut ourselves off from the vast library of man's past triumphs and mistakes, a library which offers a road map of where man has been and how he got there and which identifies those roads that lead to a dead end.

This speech is in the best tradition of the academic address. The editor and critic Hamilton Wright Mabie characterized this type as "touching deeply the feelings of the hour, stimulating its thought, awakening its conscience, and dissipating its weariness." Perhaps one of the best of this type is Ralph Waldo Emerson's "The American Scholar," delivered before the Phi Beta Kappa Society, Harvard College, August 31, 1837. Persons interested in this type of address should read John Sloan Dickey's excellent address "The Betrayal of Idealism" (REPRESENTATIVE AMERICAN SPEECHES: 1967-1968, pages 136-40) and Lester Thonssen's introduction to it.

---

[3] Text of speech delivered September 9, 1970, at opening convocation of Rockford College, Rockford, Illinois. Quoted by permission.

[4] For biographical note, see Appendix.

In 1933, the city of Chicago celebrated its centennial with a World's Fair. The theme of that fair was "A Century of Progress." All forty-eight states, a great many foreign countries and most of the major manufacturers provided a vast array of exhibits to dramatize the cultural and technological achievements of man. The millions of visitors marveled at what they saw. It is unlikely that it occurred to any of them to question the theme. Man's progress was impressive and the world had converged on Chicago to congratulate itself.

Anyone who would boast today that man had just completed a century of progress would encounter many startled responses of "A century of WHAT?" or words to that effect. The grand sweep toward an even brighter day has lost its momentum. Man is beset with so many quandaries he is not even sure which direction is forward. We have lots of things on the increase—hostilities and polarities, psychoses and neuroses, air and water impurities, an overproduction of babies—but few people would claim that these abundances or any others add up to progress.

Given the present state of affairs, man needs to put on his thinking cap and try to figure out what will make it possible for man to live with himself and with other people. All the material comforts and labor-saving devices and medical advances are to no avail if people are suffering personality disintegration as individuals and fighting each other when they are in groups. Somehow we are going to have to domesticate mankind so that he will not destroy himself individually or collectively.

It may be that the very magnitude of our difficulties will provide the impetus for more people to pay attention to the general predicament. In a recent article entitled "Vertical Is To Live—Horizontal Is To Die," Buckminster Fuller observes how the consciousness of the results of carelessness forces a person to be careful. The airplane mechanic, recognizing that lives could be endangered if he does his work sloppily, exercises the greatest care when he is performing his professional duties, but in all likelihood, at the end of the day he gets into his car and is just as foolish on the high-way as everyone else. Fuller uses the phrase, "inherent integrity of spontaneous behavior," to describe the high level of performance of air transport personnel, who automatically work with great care, conditioned as they are to the critical responsibilities they bear.

Another writer concerned with flight personnel and human behavior, Earl Hubbard, states,

It is not a question of taste—as to whether you drink or take pot or sulk. It is a question of survival. . . . The right to do as you please may be debatable in a dormitory, but it is not debatable on the frontiers of space. . . . Moral behavior is survival behavior. Moral behavior is concerned with the survival of the race of man.

Perhaps the time has come to recognize that we are really dealing with the survival of man at least as much in the dormitories as in preparing a plane for flight. People may have become so interdependent and human problems may have become so threatening that our society will not survive free-wheeling behavior on the part of the college student or the housewife or the store clerk, any more than the plane could stay in the air if the mechanics and flight engineers and pilots took such an attitude. Buckminster Fuller often refers to the earth as a spaceship. It could be that we are rapidly reaching the time when all earth dwellers are going to have to perform with the same high degree of responsibility toward each other that astronauts do in their miniature spaceships.

There is no doubt that man must discover some better ways to conduct himself. We who are blessed with the vocation of using our minds, whether temporarily involved in that vocation as students or permanently as teachers, have an extraordinary opportunity, and probably an obligation, to think our way through the troubles that lie about us and seek some more effective answers. That process requires challenging and reworking the common assumptions of our time if we are to identify and proclaim more productive ones.

This morning I wish to examine with you a very pervasive assumption that seems to underlie much of man's present activity. The assumption is that innovation is a good thing. In one of the books assigned this year for precollege reading by the entering students, *The Silent Language,* Edward Hall states, "Not only do we Americans segment and schedule time, but we look ahead and are oriented almost entirely toward the future. We like new things and we are preoccupied with change." He is right. We are preoccupied with change. The individual or the organization that is constantly springing something new not only attracts interest, but attracts allegiance as well.

Corporations which used to advertise their stability and venerability with reminders that they had been in business since 1868 or some other impressive bygone year, now wish to convey an impression of being ahead of the times. Watch the ads and you will be startled, I think, to note how many are bristling with the innovation image.

However, it isn't just the profit-making enterprises that are so inclined. Education, too, has caught the bug. College admissions literature, including our own, presents innovation as a recurrent theme, with each academic institution proclaiming itself to be a fertile source of novelty, experiment and invention. In response to the advice of the academic community, President Nixon has announced his support for the establishment of a National Academy for Higher Education which would have as one of its primary functions to serve as a clearinghouse for information about innovations which colleges and universities have undertaken. One of the newest periodicals serving higher education is entitled simply, *Change,* and features innovative theory and practice. A recent publication by the Committee for Economic Development is labeled, *The Schools and the Challenge of Innovation.* Innovation is an "in" thing. If you can outinnovate the next guy, it is presumed you are headed straight for glory.

A question poses itself. Why should anyone presume that newness, per se, is to be equated with worthiness? Why is that which is different automatically regarded as an improvement? Actually, the speed with which change is taking place has a disorienting and confusing impact upon people. John Jay Chapman vividly described this phenomenon:

> The young person . . . during the past quarter century has been like a rat in a bag which the rat-catcher keeps agitating lest the creature's teeth get a purchase on the prison. The . . . youth cannot be expected to get hold of any idea while the kaleidoscope is turning so furiously. He is numb and dizzy. He cannot connect his reading with his environment; for the books of the world have been projected out of quietude. They reflect stability, depth, relaxation, and all those conditions of peace and harmony which make thought possible. The youth, therefore, discards books as incomprehensible—foolish in fact. Education has for the time being lost its significance.

Although this excerpt is drawn from an essay more than fifty years old, it seems altogether pertinent today. The college student now is likewise beset with the circumstances of perpetual flux on campus as well as off. Even before the colleges became embroiled in the push and shove turbulence of groups pressing their demands and grievances, the colleges were emulating the outside world with new courses, new calendars, new curricula, new teaching devices and new horizons succeeding each other as swiftly as new styles in women's clothing.

It is possible that the vogue for independent study is an offshoot of the fascination with innovation. Like many other novelties, this one seems to have been accepted without critical analysis and to be carried on without meaningful evaluation. It should be ascertained, for instance, whether the aggregate learning of the students involved in independent study surpasses, equals, or is less than what would have occurred in a more formal class situation. We ought to know what are the characteristics of the student who will maximize the opportunity he has in independent study and which students will flounder on their own. A high grade-point average may not automatically signify competence for solo study. Furthermore, it needs to be asked whether the kind of learning achieved by the student gifted in independent study is worthier learning for him than what he would have achieved had he been in a class where the teacher presented a distillation of what he has found most important in his years of professional study. These questions are not intended as an assault upon independent study as a technique, which certainly has some validity, but rather as an illustration of how unthinkingly that which is new and in vogue is taken up by the academic community. In the new mythology where the innovation god sits on one of the lofty thrones, the sacrifices seem to be offered with little thought of the purposes served or the value of that which is sacrificed.

Now there may be those who perceive in these comments the setting up of a strawman to be knocked down for oratorical effect. They might assert that innovation in the current parlance is a label generally used only when the enthusiast for a particular innovation has already perceived merit in the new thing which he champions. No, I do not think that is the case. Newness *does* seem to be regarded as worthiness. Perhaps the best way to support that assertion is to turn the coin over.

Consider oldness for a moment. Of all the terms in current usage, one of the most devastating, belittling, demeaning, stop-in-the-tracksing epithets that can be applied is "reactionary." It is a red-flag word and the mere pronouncement of it tends to conjure up a vision of a dangerous, unthinking, unyielding type. And that is a paradox, for if the word does produce that result, it is an unthinking, unyielding reaction. The word, reactionary, used in a political or social context properly describes one who favors a return to former political or social policies. Surely, thinking man does not want to rule out the possibility of reinstituting policies that have proven workable in the past when successor policies have proven ineffective. Thinking man doesn't, but contemporary man blinded by the supposed virtue of innovation seems to.

Take, for instance, the swelling chorus of cries for relevance in the curriculum, and relevance in this usage seems to mean that which deals only with me, today. The relevance seeker says, "Forget all this busyness of classics and philosophy and history and literature—it doesn't reach me." Undoubtedly many who hold that attitude do so with great earnestness. Nevertheless, their views cannot be permitted to prevail in academic institutions. Lincoln was once trying a case in court. Following one of Lincoln's statements, the opposing attorney, with great indignation, snorted that he had never heard of such a thing. Lincoln replied, "Your honor, I cannot permit the distinguished counsel's ignorance, however great it may be, to take precedence over my knowledge, however limited it is."

To set aside man's recorded experience in favor of man's present gropings is upside-down logic. Although technological developments have created wholly different circumstances in which man lives, human nature seems to remain a constant. Even the most cursory review of such works as the epics of Homer, the *Book of the Dead*, the Bible and the Essays of Marcus Aurelius will establish that man's motives and man's behavior were the same several thousand years ago as they are today. With regard to human nature, the old French proverb seems on target—*"Plus ça change, plus c'est la même chose."* ("The more something changes, the more it remains the same thing.") It is, I submit, only as we can come to understand humanity that we will be better able to provide the modes of conduct and the social institutions which will make human survival possible.

To illustrate this point, let us turn to two recent analyses of two very different cultures. The first is a lecture which Dr. Walter Judd gave at Rockford College last January in which he compared the way of life of prerevolutionary China with the way of life of contemporary Western society. He observed that westerners have chosen to esteem progress, development, achievement, acquisition of things, and accumulation of power. It is a culture based on changes which are designed to increase material prosperity and to liberate man from labor and care. Our heroes are the movers and shakers, the go-getters, the businessmen and the political leaders. We

exalt youth and vigor and we put the sixty-five-year-olds out
to retirement pasture. The unit of organization is the state,
which in some Western nations is said to exist for the individual, while in other Western nations is said to be the entity for
which the individual exists.

In ancient China, by contrast, the family was the basic
unit of governance and allegiance. Any offense committed by
an individual was an offense against the people closest to the
offender, his family. The individual's sense of right and
wrong was heightened by the hurt he did to those closest to
him when he committed an offense against the commonly
held and clearly defined limits of morality. The overriding
concern of the people was not for material things or for accomplishment but for kindness and courtesy and modesty
and propriety and integrity in dealing with other human
beings. The human virtues were those which made life pleas-
anter for others. Their educational program was not designed
to make a vigorous, independent, driving go-getter out of
the child, but rather to teach him the wisdom of the past,
to arm him with the highest thoughts of the sages. Their
heroes were the contemplative scholars who had achieved
uncommon understanding about beauty and goodness. The
highest respect in each family was accorded to the eldest, so
that a person, knowing that one day those he loved the most
would count on him for his judgment, would, as a result,
strive to prepare himself in wisdom for this trust. It was a
society designed for stability, not for change. It was one in
which the meagerness of material things was offset, or really
overcome by the kindness and respect which people gave to
each other. That civilization lasted twenty-five-hundred years.

The other analysis I would call to your attention is a
work by Christopher Booker, entitled, *The Neophiliacs*. In
this volume, Mr. Booker considers what took place in Britain
from 1956 to 1969. After commenting on the headliners of
the era, the authors, musical groups, fashion experts, television personalities and the various adventures in revolt that
took place in this period, he recounts the growing disillu-

sionment with "Swinging London" and with its impact upon the lives of the people:

The lessened stature of politicians, a diminution in the general sense of community and responsibility, a feeling that life had become generally more unreal and fraught with neurosis, a widespread unease at the new power and influence of technology, a sense that too much importance was being attached to the trivial and superficial, a sense of the undoubted moral confusion that was following from the relaxation of conventional standards . . . the growth of an increasingly violent tradition of "protest" attached to so many causes that it had eventually come out in its true colors as a condition of indiscriminate rebellion.

He observes that Britain had seen the fulfillment of the two components of the twentieth century dream: "the technological dream, whereby man would achieve a golden age . . . through a complete scientific mastery of his environment," and the libertarian dream, whereby man "would at last be able to fulfill himself through the sweeping away of social and political barriers and hierarchies, through a complete understanding of his own psychology, and through the pursuit of a new and total freedom in the arts and social relationships." He notes that during this fourteen-year period there was a great acceleration in the fulfillment of both aspects of the dream, "toppling the barriers which kept the dream out of reach and therefore intact. The dream has come true . . . and its hollowness is increasingly exposed." Both technological advance and personal liberation from restraints and inhibition have proven to be hollow prizes and the society which won them is suffering the hangover of disillusionment.

In our country, the excesses of liberation have not yet run their full course, but there is here, too, a growing recognition that what has been thought to be the liberation avant-garde may, in fact, have been the trend toward a new and more devastating kind of imprisonment, that the bonds of obligation to others have been thrown off in favor of the chains of a life without hope or direction or purpose. In an article in the May issue of the *Saturday Review*, Peter Schrag laments, "To live or grow up in America in 1970 is to search for a center that doesn't exist." "The events and the forces we have created, and which we honor, tend to displace and destroy." "A generation ago . . . we regarded our discontinuities as signs of progress. Other things being equal, change was always for the better." After recognizing that that faith in change has been ill-founded, he concludes with the comment, "We are now all refugees in our own country."

All right, things are not as we would like them to be. We can sit around wringing our hands and wallowing in self-pity and some find a perverse enjoyment in doing exactly that. Or we can recognize that there has seldom been a time when the world was so ready for intelligent, highly informed courageous leadership. In a letter to the *Harvard Bulletin,* a Radcliffe graduate, Barbara Bernstein, berates two Harvard students who proclaimed that the world is over. She says,

Yes, the world is indeed sick, even in the critical ward, the nation is in the hands of Yahoos on the loose (both in and out of elective office), the problems overbearing. And what will deliver the *coup de grace?* The cop de out. It is all very sensitive and intelligent to recognize just how horrible things are, but it is sheer self-indulgence to deny any responsibility for correcting them.

If the leadership of our society is largely composed of Yahoos, then that misfortune must, in part, be attributed to an educational system which graduates Yahoos. In education, as in all other functions of our society, it may be that we have been too heavily focused on novelty and innovation and individualization, encouraging the natural instincts for aggressive experimentation in behalf of one's self and minimizing man's time-proven necessity for norms of personal conduct which the individual must accept in order for a society to work. If we permit the thrust for contemporary "relevance" to prevail, then we cut ourselves off from the vast library of man's past triumphs and mistakes, a library which offers a roadmap of where man has been and how he got there and which identifies those roads that lead to a dead end.

It is both the task and the opportunity of the liberal arts to engage in a profound scrutiny of the nature of man and to discover what has given purpose and meaning to man's life in the past and what are the accepted standards and limits which have made living together in a society bearable or even enjoyable. We must, I believe, eradicate the foolish bias which assumes that that which has been said and thought and done in the past is irrelevant and recognize that on the contrary, it is only by familiarizing ourselves with the experience of an ancient China or recent England or classical Greece and Rome that we can better interpret what is happening now and more clearly perceive the options which are open to us. The Yahoos of this generation who occupy positions of power and influence must be succeeded by people of your generation whose judgments will be formed on a broad base of specific knowledge of man's history and culture and philosophical analyses. Without such a base of humane knowledge the decisions of leadership are doomed to be determined by what is popular, or by guesswork, or we will continue to see, to quote Peter Schrag again, "those entrusted with management try to invent (or enforce) conditions and problems that make their stewardship appear successful."

Actually, we in the liberal arts colleges face a double challenge: first, to steep ourselves in the wisdom of the ages at a time when innovation and nowness have upstaged wisdom; and second, to diminish the hurly-burly of the campus scene so that our primary attentions can be directed to learning and contemplation rather than dissipated in the constant warring of power politics.

A cartoon in the *Saturday Review* last spring depicted an automobile sales area. The customer was saying to the salesman, "I drive in rush-hour traffic a lot. I need a car that can really creep." This may be an appropriate parable on which to end this commentary. Higher education has become sort of a perpetual rush-hour. Perhaps we need to acknowledge that circumstance and try to develop an educational vehicle that will shut out some of the noise and distraction on all sides, a vehicle which is not sold because of its innovation and gimmickry, but which will be intentionally designed for the slow pace of learning, which wisdom requires.

DIRECTION FOR DESTINY [5]

NOVICE G. FAWCETT [6]

Educators are generally optimists. Faced with adversity and criticism many continue to express confidence in the future constructive role of their institutions. For example, Terry Sanford, president of Duke University and former governor of North Carolina, gave an inspiring address entitled "Or Time Will Waste Us" at the fifty-third annual meeting of the American Council on Education in St. Louis, October 9, 1970. He said in part:

> We must remind the public of the ways in which its future is tied inextricably to ours. Where else in American life will we find the combination of accumulated knowledge and humanitarian concerns that will be required to devise effective solutions for the grave problems that confront us? . . .
>
> The job of those in higher education is to make the public aware of the opportunity that we all have together to convert our present crisis into a new era of human accomplishment and human accommodation. . . . We must drop our apologetic, tentative attitude, and take the positive approach. . . . Our academic performances and our research achievements can speak for themselves, but in the din and uproar of criticism, their messages won't carry beyond the campus gates. It will be up to us to carry our own message to our greater society.

Speaking with equal optimism, Novice G. Fawcett, president of the Ohio State University, addressed the Eighth Annual Dinner of the Presidents Club, a select group of supporters of his institution, on March 13, 1971. Inspirational in tone, his address gives a blueprint of what he thinks the future holds for higher education.

In the last several days, especially, some of the questions directed to me as president of this University have been formidable! When asked to name a university's most troublesome problems, I have to agree with Clark Kerr that they well

[5] Address delivered at the Eighth Annual Dinner of the Presidents Club, the Ohio State University, March 13, 1971. Quoted by permission.

[6] For biographical note, see Appendix.

may be "sex for the students, athletics for the alumni, and parking for the faculty." When asked if ever I look at the world and pray for the university, I have to be as candid as the official U.S. chaplain who admitted recently that sometimes he looked at the Senate, and prayed for the country. When asked to state one of my most routine obligations, I have to confess to professional begging. I seldom get the easy questions!

Now, if I were asked for one of our greatest but least-publicized accomplishments, I could answer by a mere wave of the hand to indicate this audience. And were someone to inquire about how it's been doing lately, my response need be only one word—wow! You, however, are destined to hear a few more words than that, which at this moment means we have even more in common than usual—to be specific—misgivings. I'm afraid I shall not get it all said; you're afraid that I shall!

Let me offer reassurance to us both. While there may be some truth in the claim that little is so outrageous that a university president won't attempt it, this one, on this occasion, recognizes two powerful deterrents. One is that the dimensions of my subject—Ohio State—are of forbidding length, breadth, scope, and complexity. The other is an audience of cherished friends, both old and new. I bow before an acknowledged impossibility in order to do right by the auditors and the academy—not to mention the orator.

No doubt you wish to know—and should be told—of progress made in attempts to dampen the conflagrations which blighted last year's springtime, a subject on which too many post-mortems have been conducted, and of the patching of cracks which often yawn between the varying ages, or shades of skin, or conflicting priorities. Well, I could cite you a whole tome, including chapter and verse, containing accounts of increased student representation in university affairs, of improved communications—both internal and external—of the rebuilt central administration, of greater faculty involvement, of the ombudsman addition, of a vastly superior police force—and of much, much more.

No doubt, for good reason, you would like to hear of the recent contributions made to mankind's knowledge-fund. Now, by taking up, in turn, each department and division of each of the sixteen colleges and the graduate school, I just might run through such an exercise—perhaps by this time tomorrow night!

You would be interested to learn—and should be made aware of—the attempts to improve the lot of society in the community, the nation, and the world. Well, for example, just last August serious work was begun to remove the guess-work from the art of interpreting foreign policy. As a result of suggestions made by Professor James Rosenau of our Social and Behavioral Sciences Laboratory, international relations specialists from campuses throughout the United States and Canada met on our campus to work toward that illuminating understanding. That's merely a start. Only by forgetting myself—and abusing you—might justice be done to a long, long list—many of them accomplishments of people in this room.

I'm not sure to which category you may assign the information that Ohio State has produced eighteen college presidents—a record exceeded only by Chicago, Columbia, Harvard, and Yale—and Yale tops us by only one. Whether this be considered as debit or credit, I'll leave up to you, but please make the decision by secret ballot!

The deliberate mention of what you're not going to hear is, I suspect, my left-handed-five-thumb effort to apply psychology. If, by now, you are thoroughly intimidated by the prospect of what might have been, you should be properly mellowed, I hope, for what is to be.

What I propose is a dram or two of the future—quite heady, and sufficiently potent for an after-dinner stimulant or an anesthetic. Since good ideas must work through the brains and will of good and farsighted people, it is essential that you be told of the thinking which guides this enterprise as it faces its next hundred years. Even though Abraham Lincoln had a point in observing that "one good thing about the future is that it comes one day at a time," tomorrow is not likely to turn out well unless, insofar as possible, each step ahead is envisioned and prepared for. Through the most recent, fresh attempt to plot the course, I have reached an awesome conclusion. Very like Edmond Rostand's now-classic avowal—except that it was in French and about love—mine is succinct, declarative, emphatic: American Higher Education Is Doing More Today But Less Than It Must Do Tomorrow. The result of such realization is an updated philosophy for the University as a whole, and for each of its parts; and, in a sense, I try it on you for size tonight.

In trying to anticipate the probable hazards which lie ahead, and to plan our way around or through the barriers of past or current construction, we find numerous spike-studded obstacles in the way of a tenable future for civilization. Overpopulation is but one of the most recognizable. Reputable demographers seem united in the conviction that no knowledgeable person expects anything but rapid future growth in people-numbers, even though the United States (in contrast to India or China or Tahiti) is now experiencing a leveling-off process which should provide this country with approximately one generation's worth of time in which to catch its breath. That span must be used in intelligent preparation for an all-but-inevitable upsurge, helped paradoxically, by such welcome advances as those made in nutrition, health, and longevity.

Lack of consideration for our nonexpandable planet has been accompanied by similar indifference to its irreplaceable natural reserves. Mankind's heedless meddling with nature, incredibly multiplied by the scientific breakthroughs and technological inventiveness of our time, has resulted in seriously dwindling and polluted resources of water, soil and air.

There is welcome promise in the possibility recently expressed at a meeting of the American Association for the Advancement of Science. Geneticist Barry Glass is of the opinion that the basic laws of life for all time to come may well have been discovered in our own lifetime, implying that science may have run out of the main unknowns. We had best hope that this be so, and that we now will focus on deriving full benefit from the headlong rush of discovery. Almost every advance still contains unlocked mysteries; too many dangers still lurk in a great deal of otherwise valuable new expertise; and too many of the world's people still receive no benefit whatsoever from a stockpile of modern miracles.

In this skeletal, very skeletal, sketch of the path ahead, there is at least one more arduous maze to be cleared—the uncertainty and confusion of a belief-system change as radical as that experienced by man in the Middle Ages. Dr. Willis Harmon of Stanford University believes that our society is now confronted by a choice between alternative societal shifts, and considers the two likeliest courses to be what he calls a "second-phase industrial society," or a "person-centered society."

My own belief is that the choice already has been made— that we are now at the last stages of a great value-system revolution. More or less simultaneously, with or without awareness of deciding, the various segments of our populace have settled on a course, passed the crossroads, and now have undertaken a collective commitment of psychic, human, and economic resources to the ideal of a person-centered society. The main, conceptual transition has been accomplished— from economic man to a less materialistic, more spiritual, intuitive, transcendental form-of-being. And the troubles we are experiencing relate to a necessary union—the fitting of new life structures and new learning systems to this new human we have chosen to become.

Reasoning based on varied and sufficiently numerous blocks of evidence, both those which are visible and those only sensed, permits me to suggest that the buffeting problems of today are not necessarily a signal of continued, accelerated change. They well may be the prelude to a period of calm. If what must be done is, then, done, humankind may achieve a golden Age of Recovery—the entree to a truly civilized civilization.

Since the Age of Reformation ushered in the Protestant ethic with its subsequent economic base, we have dealt with work-oriented man and the development of an appropriate societal structure around him. It now is necessary to accommodate a very old and recurring idealization, an addition which, at long last, may bring to mankind the quality of existence longed for throughout human experience.

The establishment of such an Age of Recovery will require a congenial atmosphere and proper accommodations, both of these stemming from much more learning, far more widely-distributed. It must have watchwords to which full weight is attached and scrupulous adherence paid. Chief among such watchwords is quality, meaning, in this context, a new sense of finiteness and limitation—the end of exponential growth in population and technology. Such dramatic changes as those of accelerating speed in travel and communications and weaponry development will have leveled off, and we must adjust to stabilized forms—making use not of the most, but of the best which is in them.

A second watchword must be balance. We constantly must be about the business of seeking a higher balance between society and self—between togetherness and individuality, between essential unity and freedom. We must be attentive to maintaining a responsible balance between man and his natural world.

The wholeness resulting from such a qualitative symmetry and stability will come through the vehicle of learning—driven by the motive power of human value. Knowledge through education will be the stuff and economy of a new person-centered society. Having succeeded in meeting an unprecedented enrollment crunch and multiple accompanying demands, higher education, with fewer distractions, can direct its steps in this direction—one toward which for some time it has been headed. Now it must take a fully cognizant, decisive lead. It must help to bring all members of our society to the fullest development of their highest potential, keenly perceptive of and sensitive to human values, keenly aware of our universal reliance on the planet which we inhabit.

Learning will extend itself over the entire life span, from infancy to final ending. It will go into the home, and the vast reaches of leisure, and the islands of industry—a union already solidified and symbolized by our Center for To-morrow. Interspersed with periods of rest, travel, work, and other pursuits we do not yet know, it will be continuous. Education will be both a moving target and a movable feast. In an unrelenting search for truth, it must be anchored to the immutable verity which Adlai Stevenson phrased in these words:

We travel together, passengers on a little spaceship, dependent on its vulnerable reserve of air and soil. We are all committed for our safety to its security and peace, and preserved from an-nihilation only by the care, the work, and the love we give our fragile craft.

With containment of population upsurge and runaway technology at fingertip reach, this country's people may be seen as completing the metamorphosis of man from new-born to youth to adult status. Physical growth eventually stops, but there is no end to the maturity of mind he may achieve.

Such learning must help us to gain what is called a "steady state"—an intelligent, tolerant, free and flexible so-ciety in which modern economics and modern technology provide the means for bringing about elimination of crucial ills and disadvantages. As the necessary alternative to ulti-mate extinction, these ends are both profitable and possible. Such Churchillian "sunlit uplands" are no longer a visionary Utopia; they are within reach. The project is not mere rhetoric; it is potential reality!

To do what must be done will take some doing! Above all else, the responsibility for delineating and reaching new national goals will require courageous, strong, established leadership by those agencies experienced in evaluating and disseminating ideas. And, most certainly, in order to maintain its fine position among that group, Ohio State will continue to rely on the understanding assistance of what's euphoniously called "the private sector." In the main, our more realistic title is "The Presidents Club."

During the course of university history, in my admittedly prejudiced opinion, not much is of greater importance than the instigation and cultivation of this invaluable nucleus of what Edgar Dale refers to as "we-centered" rather than "me-centered" citizens. Started only eight years ago by Ev Reese, Kenyon Campbell, later succeeded by Chuck Traphagan, and those of like mind, this meaningful concept of perceptive involvement, enlightened self-interest, and far-reaching humanity has made a spectacular difference, helping OSU to become one of the nation's most-productive, most-respected universities.

The effect is near-incalculable on those of us who labor here and deeply believe in what we're doing. Even so, you have the right to know at least the drift of that effect. Perhaps, since I have only myself to thank for so difficult an assignment, I can—in personal terms—make manifest the inexpressible.

More important than all else is a lifting of spirits, a strengthened resolve, the refreshment and renewal of such basic convictions as are these which I state with firm finality.

I believe in my country—in its precepts and its vigor, in the generosity and idealism and responsibility of its people.

I believe in our educational system, and in the educability of our citizens. I believe that collective wisdom can, and will, engender the knowledge and work and patience and endurance and hope which have been the glory of our past.

In the very best sense, I believe in myself, my fellow professionals and our staunch advocates. I am confident that, together, we have the know-how, the skill, and the will to see the task through.

For the Ohio State University, in which I passionately believe, for its chief spokesman, personally, and for the troubled civilization which it serves, there is only one thing more which needs be said to you— a heartfelt thank you.

In a note to his editor, penned on the flyleaf of his *East of Eden*, John Steinbeck explained that the submitted novel was a small box, carved for his friend, and that in it was placed nearly everything he had—but it still was not full. As expression of the esteem in which I hold you, I have offered my own hand-fashioned box of belief. It contains much of what I have learned during forty years in the education field and it, also, is still not full. Some hurt and much happiness are in it, and some feeling hardpressed and some heady exhilaration. A great deal of pleasure and unending challenge and hopefulness are there. And, on top of all these, are all the companionship and the gratitude and respect which I have for you. Please take it. It is offered with deep faith, and with the prayer that blessings may attend our efforts and the cause which unites us.

CURRENT ISSUES

MEDICAL CARE [1]

Thomas J. Watson, Jr. [2]

The rapid increase of medical costs, the difficulties of getting adequate service, and the persistence of health problems have been a subject of much concern. Aware of these anxieties, President Nixon included in his State of the Union Message, January 22, 1971, as his "fourth great goal . . . improving America's health care and making it available more fairly to more people." He proposed "a program to insure that no American family will be prevented from obtaining basic medical care by inability to pay."

Both the House and the Senate held hearings on the health of the nation. In March, the New York *Times* reported that four hundred members of Congress favored some type of National Health Insurance. During the first two months of the session, ten different health plans in the House and a dozen in the Senate were tossed into the hopper. Indications were that even many physicians reluctantly were coming to recognize the need for additional legislation.

Thomas J. Watson, chairman of the board of International Business Machines Corporation, presented an effective plea for a national program of medical care in a speech delivered on "Industrial Day at Mayo" at a meeting of the Mayo Foundation, Rochester, Minnesota, November 19, 1970. Among the other speakers were former President Lyndon B. Johnson. The audience included supporters of the Foundation—executives from seventy major areas and national companies.

The speech is an excellent example of a problem-solution organization. After getting attention with a series of startling statements, the speaker established his need with several well-selected facts. His solution is "some very new form of national health insurance." In the conclusion, he makes a persuasive appeal to "start now to build a bonfire of persuasion." In many ways, this address is a model of a well-conceived and well-constructed speech.

[1] Address delivered on "Industrial Day at Mayo," a meeting of the Mayo Foundation, Rochester, Minnesota, November 19, 1970.

[2] For biographical note, see Appendix.

Let me start by asking a question that this great medical center brings to mind: How would you like to live in a country which—according to the figures available in the United Nations—during the past two decades has dropped from seventh in the world to sixteenth in the prevention of infant mortality; has dropped in female life expectancy from sixth to eighth; has dropped in male life expectancy from tenth to twenty-fourth; and which has bought itself this unenviable trend by spending more of its gross national product for medical care—$1 out of every $14—than any other country on the face of the earth?

You know the country I am talking about: Our own USA, the home of the free, the home of the brave, and the home of a decrepit, inefficient, high-priced system of medical care.

Just look for a moment at what some of the figures mean. They mean that in infant mortality we have been overtaken by France, the UK, and Japan; that in male life expectancy we have been overtaken by France, Japan, West Germany and Italy.

I know experts can disagree over our precise international standing. And I realize that medical problems in the United States, Europe and Japan are not identical.

But the evidence overwhelmingly indicates that we are falling down on the job, heading in the wrong direction, and becoming as a nation a massive medical disgrace.

Now, it may seem undiplomatic to stand here under the banner of the Mayo Clinic and make an accusation like that.

I know American medicine has scored many brilliant triumphs—the magnificent record of this institution outstanding among them, including the Mayo Brothers' pioneer work in surgery; and the discovery and use of cortisone, which brought Doctors Kendall and Hench of Mayo the Nobel Prize; the work of Dr. Jonas Salk, who made one of the most significant and heartwarming discoveries in history; of Dr. Bela Schick in eliminating diphtheria; and of many others.

We have an outstanding record of individual achievement across the whole medical spectrum.

But despite all that, when I look up at the international scoreboard, I can come to only one conclusion: We are failing to fulfill adequately for all our people the first right set down in the Declaration of Independence—the right to life.

What do we have to do to restore that right to every man, every woman, every child in America?

First, as the Carnegie Commission said last month, I believe we have to beef up our arsenal: Train more doctors, more nurses, more paramedics; bail our medical and dental schools out of their present deep financial troubles; break ground for new hospitals and clinics; in a word, spend more money.

We Americans are great on that.

Show us a shortage—of airplanes or tanks or trucks or scientists or engineers or satellites—and we'll fix it.

And I believe we can do that kind of job just fine in medicine.

Second, we must build into the system better management, better organization, more incentives to increase productivity and cut inefficiency.

I find it shocking, for example, that comprehensive prepaid group practice, which has repeatedly delivered better care at lower costs, encounters legal roadblocks in more than half our states.

I find it shocking to read of Americans living in backwoods towns and city slums without a doctor or a dentist or a clinic.

I find it shocking that as 30,000 highly trained medical corpsmen return to civilian life every year—many from the field of battle—they too often discover, if they want to enter medicine as a career, that they have just one job open to them—hospital orderly.

We cannot continue to live with facts like these. We have to overhaul the system.

But as we do so, we should begin simultaneously to do the third part of the job: Put health care within reach of everyone in America.

And that means putting it within the reach of the poor.

I do not really believe, of course, that you can ever make the poor rich and the rich poor. But I do think we should have a floor for each American below which he cannot fall, and I believe this applies not only to his economic status, but also to his medical status.

For the plain fact is that under our present medical system, the poor suffer by far the most.

Moreover, if a person happens not to be white, the picture is even bleaker.

A nonwhite infant can expect to live six years less than a white infant.

The nonwhite infant mortality rate is the white rate multiplied by *two*.

The nonwhite maternal death rate is the white rate multiplied by *four*.

To me, all this adds up to a completely unacceptable situation, which I think is un-American, undemocratic and unfair.

How do we correct it, and extend coverage for medical bills to everyone?

Not just through tinkering with our present system of paying for health care.

Not just through trying to stretch the umbrella of private health insurance, which, despite its costliness, still doesn't come close to covering Americans today.

No, we need a far more thoroughgoing reform.

And that brings us up against that old taboo—"socialized medicine."

I completely believe in the American free enterprise system. But when the system clearly fails to produce a much needed good, I think we should not flinch from looking to some sort of Government intervention to get the job done.

Frequently in the past, we have faced up to such a requirement with new legislation: on workmen's compensation, child labor, the reduction of the work week, unemployment insurance, and social security.

I believe we face today the same kind of moment of truth in medicine.

And I believe we have only one choice before us that will work: some very new form of national health insurance.

Twenty-one years ago, we looked at national health insurance when President Truman urged it, and we rejected it.

And in 1949 we rejected it in part because of arguments like this which appeared that year in the June issue of the magazine of the American Medical Association under the title: "Wake up, America!"

The private profession of medicine is taking rapid strides toward the solution of this problem (of medical aid for the poor). Voluntary, prepaid hospitalization and professional insurance plans now protect 56 million Americans. . . . The American people enjoy a state of good health unequaled in the world today.

As a dyed-in-the-wool free trader, free enterpriser, and hater of bureaucracy, I accepted that argument in 1949, and I bet nearly everyone else in this room did, too.

But on the evidence—particularly the international evidence—I cannot accept it in 1970.

We need a dedicated and total effort to find a way to build a floor under each citizen of this country that assures much better quality and equality of medical services for all.

A variety of plans have been advanced to this end in the Congress, by representatives of government, labor, business and the medical profession, but none of these plans are moving very fast, and our problem is compounding.

We do not need national health insurance as a political football in 1972.

We need a new national health insurance law, and we need it now—in the next session of the Congress. Indeed, I hope the Administration will put this at the top of its priority list for 1971.

To get that legislation, the partisans of varying plans—in the Congress, the American Medical Association, the AFL-CIO—must get together and compromise their differences.

And to speed such compromise, I believe all of us as citizens—and I dare to include doctors—should start now to build a bonfire of persuasion—to speak out, to demand change, and not stop pushing for action until we get the legislation we need.

We can take pride in our system of universal public education, social security, and work laws.

The time has now arrived for us to have a system of universal public medicine in which we can also take pride.

A national program, of course, is not a panacea in itself. But as we look toward some sort of governmental approach to this problem, let us remember that the plans in Britain and the Scandinavian countries have proved very successful in keeping those countries in the front rank internationally. And certainly they have provided better medical service for all of the people than the systems they supplanted. To me, this is a tremendously compelling argument for keeping an open mind as we look for a solution.

Not long ago, on a visit to the California Institute of Technology, I read these words on a student poster: "Our age is characterized by the perfection of means and confusion of goals."

The goal before us in medicine is clear.

But we shall reach it only by doing what we have always done with our magnificent American system: fearlessly facing its faults, cutting them away, replacing them with something better, and moving on.

I think that same truth comes pounding through to us in the restless, pioneering lives of the Mayos—a truth which should guide and inspire us as we undertake the tough and crucial job which lies ahead: Bringing the fullness of American medical care to all the American people.

We must begin it now.

As the wealthiest, most powerful, best educated nation in the world—a people with a heroic history of pioneering and justice and compassion—I believe we can do no less.

WHAT THE POLICE EXPECT OF THE CITIZENRY [3]

Patrick V. Murphy [4]

The assassinations of John F. Kennedy, Robert F. Kennedy, and Martin Luther King, Jr., rudely shocked the citizenry. Many questions were raised about how these tragedies could happen in this country. Immediately questions were asked about gun laws to serve as a deterrent to crime and violence.

It is estimated that 24 million hand guns alone are in the possession of the public and that each year this number jumps 2 million. This type of weapon is involved in half the murders and two thirds of the robberies. It is not surprising, therefore, that in the past four years three presidential commissions have urged more restrictive control of guns. But last year not one of the dozens of bills restricting weapons introduced in the Congress of the United States was passed.

Police Commissioner Patrick V. Murphy of New York City argued for disarmament of the citizenry in a speech before seventy-five representatives of citizens crime commissions meeting in Washington at the Hilton Hotel, December 7, 1970. The sponsor of the meeting was the National Association of Citizens Crime Commissions, representing nineteen volunteer commissions, including those in Chicago, Philadelphia, New York, and New Orleans.

In the seventh paragraph of the talk Mr. Murphy gives his proposition: "Let us take the guns away from the people." The New York *Times* (December 8, 1970) reported that in his oral presentation he deleted from that same paragraph the following sentence: "And I would look forward to the day when it would not be necessary for policemen to carry a sidearm." He explained later that he omitted this sentence because he did not want to be misunderstood to imply that he favored "disarming of police."

Although it is not eloquent, the speech presents a forthright view of the issue which plagues the country. The National Rifle Association, a powerful lobby, will no doubt continue to argue the negative vigorously and to fight any effort to restrict ownership of weapons.

[3] Address delivered at meeting of National Association of Citizens Crime Commissions, Hilton Hotel, Washington, D.C., December 7, 1970. Quoted by permission.

[4] For biographical note, see Appendix.

Thank you for inviting me to join you today. I am delighted to be here among friends and colleagues who share a common interest in crime prevention. The topic you have asked me to explore"—What the Police Expect Of the Citizenry"—is both fascinating and encouraging to me.

It is a refreshing departure from the traditional topic where the subject places the police on the defensive, and we are asked to explain and justify increasing crime rates. Perhaps we can sharpen the focus of our discussion by paraphrasing the eloquent expression of the late President John F. Kennedy: Ask not what your police can do for you but ask what you can do for your police.

The law in our society is predicated on the theory of voluntary compliance. It is the same philosophy applied by the Internal Revenue Service where the citizen is expected to report honestly his income and voluntarily pay his taxes. This has become our way of life, and it is universally accepted in varying degrees.

An interesting case recently came to our attention. It involved a taxpayer who sent a money order of $100 to the Collector of Internal Revenue with an anonymous note explaining that he had cheated on his tax return five years ago, and his conscience bothered him ever since. There was also a postscript which stated, "If my conscience still bothers me I will send you the balance."

The police service relies on the theory that we are essentially an honest and peaceful society, and that most people voluntarily comply with the law. The presumption that we are a peace-loving people may be a fallacy. It was little more than a hundred years ago when we were still a frontier nation pioneering in the wilderness. In the span of history it was only yesterday when shotguns rode the horsedrawn vehicles and every householder was armed. The stagecoach has disappeared but the deadly firearm is still with us: with an estimated hundred million guns in the hands of private citizens. We are a more sophisticated people today, enjoying greater material comforts, yet we have failed to rise above our violent heritage. We have failed to achieve domestic tranquillity, and we are confronted daily with violence by gunfire.

Studies on guns—long and short—abound. Numerous laws on the national, state and local level limit the manufacture, sale, importation and possession of firearms. And yet there is no diminution in their unlawful use. Under the deceptive guise of freedom and the belief that citizens must be armed to resist tyranny, the American people tolerate and abet assault, robbery, murder and street crime at gunpoint. If this is freedom in its finest form, it is also freedom in its final hour. We have no way of determining how many firearms are in violent hands. We don't know the extent of the condition but we know the condition exists. Throughout the country in recent years tons of weapons have been plundered in transit and stolen from armories and gun dealers.

We are beyond the stage of restrictive licensing and uniform laws. We are at that point in time and terror when nothing short of a strong uniform policy of domestic disarmament will alleviate the danger which is crystal clear and perilously present. Let us take the guns away from the people. Exemptions should be limited to the military, the police and those licensed for good and sufficient reason.

Thousands of suicides, accidental deaths, slayings of relatives or acquaintances and the tragic list of assassinations in our time may never have been if the lethal instrument of death were not so readily available, and if the firearm as contraband had been the accepted national mode.

Let us ask ourselves the hard questions: Do we as a people really abhor violence? We are obviously concerned about crime. But to what extent? Perhaps our feelings about violence are not as strong as we think. With the increasing incidence of crime there has been a sharp rise in the number of people who obtain weapons for self-defense. It is reminiscent of the era of the armed frontiersman, but the dangerous difference is that the sparse frontier has given way to heavily populated urbania. I leave to your imagination the tragic consequence of a shot fired in a downtown shopping area or even on a neighborhood street.

For too long we have indulged the gun maniacs. The name of the game is human life, and it is a game we dare not play. The stakes are too high for an advanced society which values human life above all other considerations.

We are a proud people with a proud heritage. Out of the undeveloped wilderness that was once America, we have overdeveloped this vast region to the extent that pollution affects our streams and our waterways and contaminates the air we breathe. The conservationists tell us wild life is disappearing, too. With the development of formerly rural areas to accommodate the growing population, the sportsman's field is receding and his targets are diminishing.

As a people, Americans are singularly distinguished for their record of achievement. But we have failed to plan for the debilitating byproducts that accompany progress. This is well illustrated by our ecological problems. It is common knowledge to the doctor and chemist that the development of a new and helpful drug requires careful observation of the patient to ascertain the possibility of contraindications. Sometimes the resultant side effects may be more hazardous than the original malady which the new drug was designed to cure. This is the pattern of unenforceable statutes which generate contempt rather than confidence in our system of justice. We have such laws on our books.

Within the province of police enforcement I would like to see fewer regulatory laws. The policeman would be a more effective crime-fighter, and he would be held in higher public esteem, if he were not required to enforce so many regulations which attempt to control morals—the so-called victimless crimes. By charging our police with the responsibility to enforce the unenforceable we subject them to disrespect and corruptive influences. And we provide the organized criminal syndicates with illicit industries upon which they thrive.

The tremendous progress we have made has been accompanied by an astonishing record of tragic and abysmal failure. Crime has been increasing for many years. And let us not delude ourselves, it will continue to rise. The criminal mind will not repent. Criminal activities will not relent. Crime is woven into the fabric of our society. Crime will not abate when housing and education are inadequate, when there is widespread unemployment, when there is inequality of opportunity, when there is a woeful lack of full citizenship rights, when affluence and poverty live side by side.

George Bernard Shaw once wrote that security cannot exist where the danger of poverty hangs over everyone's head. Poverty degrades the poor and infects with its degradation the whole neighborhood in which they live. And whatever can degrade a neighborhood can degrade an entire civilization. In this context poverty is a burden not only on the poor but also on the affluent and on every intermediate level of our social and economic structure.

Mr. Shaw was a man of great vision. Without stating the time and place, and without specific reference to narcotics, his words vividly describe the spread of drug addiction. In our cities it began amid poverty in the ghetto. And the contagion spread into the more prosperous upper-class neighborhoods. The monetary cost of addiction in terms of goods stolen by addicts in their desperation to feed their craving for drugs has been estimated in astronomical figures. It is a cost that small businessmen, car owners, householders and every productive citizen has had to pay. Even the poverty-stricken are not immune from the frantic depredations of the addict in need of money to satisfy his craving for drugs. Addicts remain close to their home areas and it is the people in those areas who are most victimized by drug-related crime. The drain on society is reflected in the wasted lives of the addicts themselves and the predatory pursuit in the subculture of the addict world. It began with poverty. It infected the poor neighborhoods and the degradation has spread through an entire civilization—just as George Bernard Shaw once wrote.

Crime will not abate while the increasing arrest rate is paralleled by increasing recidivism. Crime will flourish as long as men are incarcerated in penal institutions which fail to rehabilitate. The national recidivism rate has been estimated at upwards of 90 per cent. This means that at least nine of every ten men who leave prison eventually return to crime. And the full cycle begins again in the overcrowded prison with its inadequate personnel and poorly designed facilities which provide a fertile breeding ground for criminal proclivity.

The breakdown in our system of criminal justice is reflected not only in the operation of our correctional institutions but, also, in the parole and probation services; in the failing efforts of the prosecution, and in legal maneuvers in the courtroom. Today there is as much time spent in the courtroom arguing motions as in conducting the actual trial itself. The bench and bar have become afflicted with a kind of "motion sickness."

This brings to mind a story involving Charles Evans Hughes when he was Chief Justice of the Supreme Court. He had taken several of his associates on a cruise down Chesapeake Bay. It was a bright clear day but the water was choppy, and the late Justice Cardozo became violently ill. Mr. Hughes found him leaning over the rail, his complexion a sickly green. "I'm sorry," said the chief justice. "Is there anything I can do for you?" With great effort Justice Cardozo raised his head and muttered: "Yes, please, overrule this terrible motion."

When the last preliminary motion is made and argued and ruled upon, the trial commences. But, again, there are delays *ad nauseam*. The appalling waste of time severely weakens the deterrent effect of our criminal law, and it breeds contempt for the law. Under our system of justice it is not uncommon for four or five years to elapse from the time of arrest to final disposition. The unreasonable excesses of our criminal procedures can—and must—be eliminated. With protracted hearings, motions, appeals, pretrial and posttrial delays, our system of criminal justice is quickly grinding to a dead halt. We attempt to be fair to the defendant but, in effect, we violate his rights under the Sixth Amendment by failing to guarantee a speedy trial.

With an ever-increasing number of arrests and increasing delays in the courtroom we are further crowding congested court calendars and complicating the work of understaffed court personnel: to the extent that our system of criminal justice is losing public respect. There is a growing lack of public confidence and, ironically, the uniformed patrolman is first to feel the harsh effects of an alienated public. Without public respect and confidence and cooperation, the policeman is placed under a severe handicap which adds to the complexities of his arduous duties.

To function effectively the police must have the cooperation of every citizen. The community itself cannot remain neutral on the theory that the police are paid to do the job, and the police alone are the public protectors. Law enforcement is everybody's business. Public safety on the street and in the home requires a total commitment; not only of the police, the courts, the district attorneys, the correction, parole and probation services, but also of the community as a whole. The problem of crime starts long before the police are involved. And—unfortunately—it continues long after the police function, culminating in arrest, has been performed.

If crime were purely a police matter there would be little criminal activity. With improved police training and the application of sophisticated technical devices we are seeing a corresponding increase in police effectiveness. Our men are intelligent, responsible and humane public servants —skilled practitioners in the art of dealing with people. Yet crime proliferates. Let us not fault the police for the conditions which breed crime: poverty, illiteracy, ill health, slum housing and limited opportunity for those most in need of opportunity.

We can deplore. We can discuss recommendations as we are doing today. But we cannot sweep the causes of crime under the rug. It is a contagion that will surface and spread. Social change is needed. In its present form it is a barrier to peace and tranquillity. Through social change, we must remove not only the causes of crime but, also, the deadly instrument of violence. Let us repair the breakdown in criminal justice through speedier trials. Let us remove the unenforceable law from the sphere of police enforcement. Let us also develop a rehabilitation system that rehabilitates and does not return the offender to prison.

It may seem an unusual suggestion for a police commissioner to make to members of crime commissions—but perhaps one of the most helpful things citizens can do to help us is to demand that the current "nonsystem" of criminal justice be developed into a system. As part of that demand the question must be posed: Is the crime-control dollar being spent most effectively in our cities? Is any one part of the system—police, prosecution, courts, corrections—receiving an excessive share of available fiscal resources to the disadvantage of one or more of the other parts? Such imbalance only weakens the potential of the whole system.

This is what the citizen can do for police. The policeman asks for a reasonable climate in which he can function effectively. He asks for public acceptance, not accolades. In a street problem the citizen is asked to accept the policeman's leadership, trust his judgment, heed his words, and give him the respect and esteem so necessary—so vital—to the dangerous task of policing our cities. Together, the citizen and the policeman can attain that human quality—that majestic quality of mankind—that eludes our society.

A GREAT VOICE . . . SILENCED

A PROMISE MADE, A PROMISE TO KEEP: WHITNEY YOUNG AND THE NATION [1]

JAMES E. CHEEK [2]

The death of Whitney Young, Jr., Executive Director of the National Urban League, March 11, 1971, robbed the nation of the leadership of one of the foremost black leaders of the civil rights movement. For the ten years that he served as director of the League, he worked strenuously and effectively to gain favorable opportunities for black Americans. While others sought to stir hostility and rebellion, Young attempted to gain his goal through working within the system with the leaders in business, labor, and government. *Newsweek* (March 22, 1971) said of his effort: "He was Mr. Inside to the black revolution—a cool, urbane diplomat whose work began where the street marches and the picket lines left off."

Mr. Young in his own right was an effective speaker (see his speech "The Crisis of the Cities: The Danger of the Ghetto," REPRESENTATIVE AMERICAN SPEECHES: 1966-1967, pages 82-104). Before the 1970 National Urban League Conference, New York City, July 19, 1970, he expressed his philosophy (see *Vital Speeches of the Day*, September 15, 1970, pages 732-6) :

> The proud black spirit seeks justice and decency. It seeks to move beyond racism to a new era of progress and reconciliation. It seeks power not for its own sake, but in order to use it wisely and to prevent its misuse by racism. It seeks peace with honor, justice with respect. It seeks a newer world, and a better tomorrow.

Dr. James E. Cheek, President of Howard University, delivered a fitting and inspirational eulogy on Whitney Young, Jr. at a special memorial service held at the Bibleway Church, Washington, D.C., March 19, 1971. As the speaker suggests, the speech is more than a eulogy; it is a plea to continue the program of

[1] Address delivered at special memorial service, sponsored by the Washington Urban League, at Bibleway Church, March 19, 1971. Quoted by permission.

[2] For biographical note, see Appendix.

Whitney Young, Jr. Dr. Cheek revealed this purpose as follows: "I should like . . . to say something not so much about Whitney, but rather more about the nation—the nation he loved, the society in whose possibilities he believed."

Since last Thursday, March 11, 1971, when the news of Whitney Young's death was flashed around the world, so many words have been said about him and his life and work, that further utterances of this kind in this memorial service would be anticlimactic. He has been eulogized and buried; we must try to memorialize him.

I should like in these brief moments, therefore, to say something not so much about Whitney, but rather more about the nation— the nation he loved, the society in whose possibilities he believed.

For we mourn in this time not Whitney. We need not mourn for him, but we should mourn for the nation. Whitney did what he could. But the nation has not done all it could or all it ought to do.

Whitney believed in equality; but the nation practices inequality.

Whitney believed in justice; but the nation practices injustice.

Whitney believed in fraternity; but the nation practices division.

Whitney believed in an open society; but the nation practices a closed society.

Whitney believed in freedom and liberty; but the nation practices oppression and repression.

Almost two centuries ago this nation in its struggle to become born made a promise; it still has this promise to keep.

Whitney Young lived and labored in an effort to help his country keep its promise in his lifetime. He believed to the end in the possibilities of a nation whose doctrine and deeds transcended racism; whose essential character did not depend upon color of skin, or accent of language, or origin of nation, or of professions of religion. But whose essential character was to be shaped and made by the devotion of its citizens to the love of liberty, the practice of justice and the recognition of equality; a nation whose citizens lived in fraternity, one with the other.

For what Whitney believed in was what America promised when it was born in 1776. But America is now almost two centuries old; it continues to make the promise, but it also continues to find ways not to keep it.

We do not know the eloquence of a great voice until that voice has been silenced. We do not feel the power of a great spirit until that spirit has been stilled. The eloquence of Whitney Young's voice is heard now in its silence; the power of his spirit is now felt in its stillness.

He is gone and we are here. Whitney Young is dead. But the nation continues to live. We, who are left behind, cannot bring Whitney Young back to life again; but we who are left behind can prevent the nation he struggled for from dying.

Perhaps it cannot be said of Whitney Young that he died *to make* men free. But in truth it can be said, he died *while* trying to make both men and this nation free.

No words spoken here or elsewhere can adequately pay tribute to his life or to the memory of that life. He, in fact, believed that men were to be judged not by what they *said*, but by what they *did*.

It is not important now what the nation says about Whitney's life. It is important now what the nation does about Whitney's work. His life cannot be restored, but his work can be continued and brought to fulfillment.

We shall hear no more that voice we now know to have been eloquent. We shall experience no longer that spirit we now know to have been powerful.

But we—as a nation—can keep the voice eloquent and we can keep that spirit powerful not by continuing to quote from Whitney's speeches and his books and not by continuing to recall interesting and important anecdotes about his life. The eloquence of his voice can be heard and the power of his spirit can be felt if the nation would now decide to create for Whitney Young a monument. A monument, not of stone or of bronze, but a monument fashioned of Whitney's dream, carved out of his hope, and shaped in the form of what he called "the domestic Marshall Plan." And let it be called the "Whitney Young Plan" embodying not only his name and his spirit, but also his program, his goals, his objectives.

And through the Whitney Young Plan, let this nation become that "Open Society" for which he struggled, and through the Whitney Young Plan, let this nation move— in this decade—beyond racism.

And in this decade, let this nation use its resources and its institutions not only to land men on the moon, but on earth to stand men on their feet.

And in this decade, let this nation do for Americans what it claims to champion for the Vietnamese: human freedom and human dignity.

And in this decade, let this nation do for American cities what it did in the past two decades for foreign nations: destroy the ghettoes and the slums; rebuild the schools and reinvigorate the human spirit.

And in this decade, let this nation now begin to seek for itself what it seeks for the world: not only a generation of world peace, but more than a generation of racial peace and racial goodwill.

And let these things be done by Americans, on behalf of America, in the interest of Americans. Not because it is expedient, but because it is right. Not because it is our wish, but because it is our duty; and not because of our desire for world power, but because of our determination to keep a historic promise.

And if we the people—the nation—are not willing or capable of doing these things, let us now say so. Let us, before the world, throw down the gauntlet and say: We do not believe in equality, we do not believe in justice, we do not believe in fraternity. Let us make clear to ourselves and to the world that this America will exploit as other nations have exploited. That we shall continue to oppress as other nations have oppressed. That we believe in the necessity of the few ruling the many and that we are determined that white men shall dominate black men, and that we are prepared—as a nation—to renounce the promise we made almost two centuries ago and to take our chances with the laws of history and with the laws of history's sovereign God.

And if this be the nation's choice and the nation's decision, then let those who walked with Whitney, who talked with him, who organized with him, who cried with him, who believed with him, who hoped with him, who planned with him say to our country—the land of our birth—that we believe with Whitney that James Russell Lowell spoke eternal truth when he wrote:

> The laws of changeless justice bind
> Oppressor with oppressed.
> And sure as sin and suffering joined
> We march to fate abreast.

Almost two centuries ago, this Republic at the moment of its birth made a promise, it still has a promise to keep.

Whitney Young labored for two decades to help the nation keep its promise. Those whom Whitney has left behind do not have two decades remaining. The dateline of American history is built around his grave. His departure is a watershed in our national experience.

He is dead, but we are alive. And if we have in fact not paid our final respects to him in laying to rest his body, let us not now pay our final respects to him in laying to rest his work.

THE GOVERNORS SPEAK

THE INAUGURAL ADDRESS [1]

Cecil D. Andrus [2]

In at least thirty-five states, governors were elected during the fall of 1970. In some instances, these contests stirred more attention and required more effort than some of the contests for national offices. Certainly a state governor faces perplexing problems.

The inaugural address, a type of ceremonial speech, provides the governor with an opportunity to seek unity and support and to announce his future programs. Too often what a governor says receives and deserves little attention and is not long remembered. On schedule, the recipient delivers his speech because custom dictates he must. As a result, a governor seldom achieves anything approaching eloquence; too often what he says is filled with trite language and overworked stereotypes.

An exception to the usual speeches is the inaugural address of Cecil D. Andrus of Idaho, delivered on the statehouse steps in Boise, January 4, 1971. Governor Andrus, who in 1960 had been the youngest senator ever elected to the Idaho legislature, was in 1970 the first Democratic governor to be elected in Idaho in twenty-four years. Optimistic and catching the spirit of the West, the Idaho governor urges that "the quality of life" be improved through attention to the people's welfare and natural resources of the state. He echoes a national concern when he says:

> The decade of the seventies is a time to speak out and insist that the enemy within is not the young of America. Rather, the enemy is many things: mismanagement of government and resources, disease, poverty, inadequate education, shrinking employment, and other ills that afflict our society.

Coming from a state that has produced Senators William E. Borah and Frank Church, Governor Andrus had good models to follow and inspiration to eloquence.

---

[1] Text delivered at Boise, Idaho, January 4, 1971. Quoted by permission.
[2] For biographical information, see Appendix.

Mr. Chief Justice; Governor Samuelson; distinguished members of the Idaho legislature; reverend clergy; my fellow citizens:

More than a century has passed since a courageous band of frontier legislators assembled near the confluence of two mighty rivers, and established Idaho's first governing body.

It was at Lewiston in 1863 that Idaho began its quest for greatness.

Today, 107 years later, we are still pursuing that original dream—the dream that all men might find a good life in a most splendid state called Idaho.

We must never lose sight of our early leaders' courageous goals. In 1971 we must continue to pursue that quest for greatness so that our accomplishments in the 1970s will be the bedrock of hope for our people in the 1980s and for all time to come.

The quality of life for all in Idaho is our goal. Therefore, it is time to rise up and draw the guidelines for the future. We must prepare now, more carefully than ever before, to preserve and improve what is ours and ours alone.

The quality of life has many meanings for our family of Idaho citizens. For some it is the comfort of faith in our ability to cope with the problems of the day. For others it is a responsive government . . . or a relevant education.

Quality of life for many is the treasured resource of silence abundant in our forests and along the shores of mountain lakes.

By focusing our attention and ability in a positive vein, by recognizing the good and desiring to make the good better, we can create a better life and a better state for Idaho and her wholesome people.

Although having passed the century mark in age and wisdom, Idaho remains in its infancy and holds the potential for social and economic maturity unmatched by those around us.

While these are trying times for our people who want to know what the future will bring and how they can influence the course of events, we can face the future with confidence *if—if* we are willing to recognize that our strength as a unique community of people lies in our own diversity.

We can be masters of our destiny—*if* we realize that among us are men and women of many talents and that those talents can be utilized for the betterment of all.

We can face the coming years with understanding—*if* we realize that diversity need not pit generation against generation, farmer against city dweller, region against region.

And, we can work together in common cause—*if* we believe that when one among us is in need, we are all in need and when one among us succeeds, we all succeed.

However, we must be patient to remake, to redesign and to rebuild. All will not be done easily or quickly.

Let us have the same spirit John F. Kennedy had in 1961 when he faced the problems and the people and said:

"All this will not be finished in the first 100 days. Nor will it be finished in the first 1,000 days, nor in the life of this Administration, nor even perhaps in our lifetime on this planet. But let us begin."

Idaho is still a wilderness. It remains a magnificent portrait of the America our forefathers discovered and settled.

Idaho still has land where no man has ventured, where no machine has left its ugly scar. Idaho has water so clear and air so pure they are but dreams in the minds of most men.

We must take great pride in our natural wealth and heritage, but we must guard against letting this pride lull us into false complacency.

We are independent people, we Idahoans, and we must remain independent to provide protection for our gentle surroundings. We can and must make certain that our natural resources are developed for the benefit of all in Idaho and in a way that our precious lands are not smeared, our air befouled and our water dirtied.

We must recognize that we have not been as attentive as we should have been to the hazards of an industrial age. In part, our environment does show signs of blight.

We could reflect on the days of the past when all was new, all was clean and all was unmarred by man. But this is not a time for looking back. We cannot begin anew with the traditional methods that have brought us to where we are today.

I propose a new beginning. We must assemble a dedicated team to rewrite traditions, to redesign methods of achievement and to remake the ravaged lands we have so brutally abused.

The decade of the seventies is a time to speak out and insist that the enemy within is not the young of America. Rather, the enemy is many things: mismanagement of government and resources, disease, poverty, inadequate education, shrinking employment and other ills that afflict our society.

During the decade of the seventies we must address ourselves to what unites us rather than to what divides us. There are those who would tear down the state and nation, or more popularly, burn it down. Instead we must gather ourselves together to improve rather than destroy.

If there is any burning to be done, let us burn the clichés that have kept us from each other, kept us from forming a grand alliance against empty pockets, empty stomachs and empty minds.

I agree with a great Democrat, Thomas Jefferson, who said he liked the dreams of the future rather than the history of the past.

We have now opened a new era with a cry for change. We have gone before the people and asked for their judgment and their judgment has borne us out.

Since the mark we place upon this state will endure a generation or more, the decade of the seventies can be a decade of rebirth. We can examine our government, our schools, our economy and ourselves. We can retain and make better the good and the sound. We can repair that which needs repairing and replace that which needs replacing.

But, leadership is only half the answer. The quality of life in Idaho depends on you. If you want quality, you will have it, for in the final analysis it is the people who must meet the challenge of the future. It is our people, together, who control the destiny of Idaho.

Today, as we stand together before God, our country and our state, let us pledge to undertake a mission of energy and courage to renew Idaho for ourselves and for our children.

With guidance from the Almighty, with the spirit of youth and the insight of age, we can and we will face the future with hope rather than fear.

INAUGURATION ADDRESS [3]

JIMMY CARTER [4]

During the fall elections, moderate youthful governors were elected in South Carolina, Georgia, Florida, and Arkansas. After interviewing two of these Southerners, Jimmy Carter of Georgia and John C. West of South Carolina, Tom Wicker of the New York *Times* (April 25, 1971) wrote:

> Both governors described themselves as products of a particular time and mood in the South, rather than as creators of a movement. As they see it, the people of most of the southern states are not only tired of the struggle to maintain old racial customs but are convinced that the battle is irrevocably lost. Not happily, but with a sense of inevitability they want to get on to other matters that, anyway, are coming to seem more important.

In his inaugural address, delivered January 12, 1971, in Atlanta, Governor Jimmy Carter approached his term with refreshing frankness about solving the problems of his state. He attracted national attention when he declared:

> I say to you quite frankly that the time for racial discrimination is over. . . . No poor, rural, weak, or black person should ever have to bear the additional burden of being deprived of the opportunity of an education, a job, or simple justice.

Governor Maddox and other fellow Georgians:

It is a long way from Plains to Atlanta. I started the trip four and a half years ago and, with a four year detour, I finally made it. I thank you all for making it possible for me to be here on what is certainly the greatest day of my life. But now the election is over, and I realize that the test of a man is not how well he campaigned, but how effectively he meets the challenges and responsibilities of the office.

---

[3] Address delivered January 12, 1971, in Atlanta, Georgia. Quoted by permission.

[4] For biographical note, see Appendix.

I shall only take a few minutes today to summarize my feelings about Georgia. Later this week my program will be described in some detail in my State of the State and Budget messages to the house and senate.

I am grateful and proud to have with us the Naval Academy Band, because it reminds me as it did when I was a midshipman of the love of our nation and of its goals and ideals. Our country was founded on the premise that government continually derives its power from independent and free men. If it is to survive, confident and courageous citizens must be willing to assume responsibility for the quality of our Government at any particular time in history.

This is a time for truth and frankness. The next four years will not be easy ones. The problems we face will not solve themselves. They demand from us the utmost in dedication and unselfishness from each of us. But this is also a time for greatness. Our people are determined to overcome the handicaps of the past and to meet the opportunities of the future with confidence and with courage.

Our people are our most precious possession and we cannot afford to waste the talents and abilities given by God to one single Georgian. Every adult illiterate, every school dropout, every untrained retarded child is an indictment of us all. Our state pays a terrible and continuing human and financial price for these failures. It is time to end this waste. If Switzerland and Israel and other people can eliminate illiteracy, then so can we. The responsibility is our own, and as Governor, I will not shirk this responsibility.

At the end of a long campaign, I believe I know our people as well as anyone. Based on this knowledge of Georgians north and south, rural and urban, liberal and conservative, I say to you quite frankly that the time for racial discrimination is over. Our people have already made this major and difficult decision, but we cannot underestimate the challenge of hundreds of minor decisions yet to be made. Our inherent human charity and our religious beliefs will be taxed to the limit. No poor, rural, weak, or black person should ever have to bear the additional burden of being deprived of the opportunity of an education, a job or simple justice. We Georgians are fully capable of making our own judgments and managing our own affairs. We who are strong or in positions of leadership must realize that the responsibility for making correct decisions in the future is ours. As governor, I will never shirk this responsibility.

Georgia is a state of great natural beauty and promise, but the quality of our natural surroundings is threatened because of avarice, selfishness, procrastination and neglect. Change and development are necessary for the growth of our population and for the progress of our agricultural, recreational, and industrial life. Our challenge is to insure that such activities avoid destruction and dereliction of our environment. The responsibility for meeting this challenge is our own. As governor, I will not shirk this responsibility.

In Georgia, we are determined that the law shall be enforced. Peace officers must have our appreciation and complete support. We cannot educate a child, build a highway, equalize tax burdens, create harmony among our people, or preserve basic human freedom unless we have an orderly society. Crime and lack of justice are especially cruel to those who are least able to protect themselves. Swift arrest and trial and fair punishment should be expected by those who would break our laws. It is equally important to us that every effort be made to rehabilitate law breakers into useful and productive members of society. We have not yet attained these goals in Georgia, but now we must. The proper function of a government is to make it easy for man to do good and difficult for him to do evil. This responsibility is our own. I will not shirk this responsibility.

Like thousands of other businessmen in Georgia, I have always attempted to conduct my business in an honest and efficient manner. Like thousands of other citizens, I expect no less of government.

The functions of government should be administered so as to justify confidence and pride.

Taxes should be minimal and fair.

Rural and urban people should easily discern the mutuality of their goals and opportunities.

We should make our major investments in people, not buildings.

With wisdom and judgment we should take future actions according to carefully considered long-range plans and priorities.

Governments closest to the people should be strengthened, and the efforts of our local, state and national governments need to be thoroughly coordinated.

We should remember that our state can best be served by a strong and independent governor, working with a strong and independent legislature.

Government is a contrivance of human wisdom to provide for human wants. Men have a right to expect that these wants will be provided by this wisdom.

The test of a government is not how popular it is with the powerful and privileged few, but how honestly and fairly it deals with the many who must depend upon it.

William Jennings Bryan said, "Destiny is not a matter of chance, it is a matter of choice. Destiny is not a thing to be waited for, it is a thing to be achieved."

Here around me are seated the members of the Georgia legislature and other state officials. They are dedicated and honest men and women. They love this state as you love it and I love it. But no group of elected officers, no matter how dedicated or enlightened, can control the destiny of a great state like ours. What officials can solve alone the problems of crime, welfare, illiteracy, disease, injustice, pollution, and waste? This control rests in *your* hands, the people of Georgia.

In a democracy, no government can be stronger, or wiser, or more just than its people. The idealism of the college student, the compassion of a woman, the common sense of the businessman, the time and experience of a retired couple, and the vision of political leaders must all be harnessed to bring out the best in our state.

As I have said many times during the last few years, I am determined that at the end of this administration we shall be able to stand up anywhere in the world—in New York, California, or Florida and say "I'm a Georgian"—and be proud of it.

I welcome the challenge and the opportunity of serving as governor of our state during the next four years. I promise you my best. I ask you for your best.

APPENDIX

BIOGRAPHICAL NOTES

ANDRUS, CECIL D. (1931-). Born, Hood River, Oregon; student, Oregon State University, 1948-49; member, Idaho senate, 1961-66, 1969-70; governor of Idaho, 1971- ; state general manager, Paul Revere Life Insurance Company, 1969-70; served with the United States Navy, 1951-55; named honor man of the recruit company; active in community affairs, Orofino, Idaho; defeated as Democratic gubernatorial candidate, 1966.

BURGER, WARREN EARL (1907-). Born, St. Paul, Minnesota; studied at University of Minnesota, 1925-27; LL.B., magna cum laude, St. Paul College of Law (now William Mitchell College of Law) ; Doctor of Laws, William Mitchell College of Law; honorary degrees, LL.D., William Mitchell College of Law and New York University; admitted to Minnesota bar, 1931; partner, Faricy, Burger, Moore and Costello (and predecessor firms), 1935-53; faculty, William Mitchell College of Law, 1931-48; assistant attorney general in charge of Civil Division, United States Department of Justice, 1953-56; judge of U.S. Court of Appeals of District of Columbia, 1956-69; Chief Justice of the United States, 1969- ; lecturer, American and European law schools; faculty, Appellate Judges Seminar, New York University Law School, 1958- ; member and legal adviser to United States delegation to the International Labor Organization in Geneva, 1954; contributor to law journals and other publications. (See also *Current Biography, November 1969*.)

CARTER, JIMMY (1924-). Born, Plains, Georgia; attended Georgia Institute of Technology; graduate, United States Naval Academy, Annapolis; postgraduate instruction in nuclear physics; served in United States Navy; served two terms in Georgia senate (voted most effective member); past president, Georgia Planning Association; first chairman, West Central Georgia Planning and Development Commission; former chairman, Sumter County Board of Education; district governor, Lions International; state

chairman, March of Dimes; governor of Georgia (Democrat),
1971- .

CHEEK, JAMES EDWARD (1932-). Born, Roanoke Rapids,
North Carolina; B.A., Shaw University, 1955; B.D., Colgate-Roch-
ester Divinity School, 1958; Ph.D., Drew University, 1962; in-
structor in western history, Union Junior College, 1959-61; assistant
professor of New Testament and historical theology, Virginia
Union University, 1961-63; president, Shaw University, 1963-69;
Howard University, 1969- ; special consultant to President Nixon,
May-June, 1970; member of President's Commission on Campus
Unrest, June-October 1970; Fund for the Advancement of Theolog-
ical Education; National Association for Equal Opportunity in
Higher Education; Greater Washington Educational Television
Association; Educational Policy Center, Inc.

CHURCH, FRANK (1924-). Born, Boise, Idaho; on debating
team, Boise high school; A.B., Stanford University, 1947; LL.B.,
1950; admitted to Idaho bar, 1950; practiced law in Boise, 1950-56;
chairman, Crusade for Freedom, 1954, 1955; keynote speaker, state
Democratic convention, 1952; United States Senate (Democrat,
Idaho), 1956- ; keynote speaker, Democratic National Convention, 1960; first lieutenant, World War II; one of ten outstanding
young men, United States Junior Chamber of Commerce, 1957;
recipient, American Legion Oratorical Contest Award, 1941 ("The
American Way of Life"); Joffre Debate Medal, Stanford University,
1947; Phi Beta Kappa; member, Senate Committee on Foreign
Relations; Committee on Interior and Insular Affairs. (See also
Current Biography: March 1958.)

FAWCETT, NOVICE G. (1909-). Born, Gambier, Ohio; B.S.,
magna cum laude, Kenyon College, 1931; M.A., Ohio State University, 1937; postgraduate work, Ohio State University, 1943-47;
honorary degrees from many universities, including Kent State
University, Miami (Ohio) University, and the University of Cin-
cinnati; teacher, Gambier (Ohio) high school, 1931-34; superin-
tendent of schools of several Ohio school systems, including Akron
and Columbus, 1934-56; president, Ohio State University, 1956- ;
member, scholarship board, Ford Motor Company Fund Scholarship Program; president and other offices of the National Associa-

tion of State Universities and Land-Grant Colleges, 1962-67; president, Ohio College Association, 1966-67; other education organizations; Phi Beta Kappa; Kappa Phi Kappa; 33° Mason; past director, Ohio Council on Economic Education.

HESBURGH, THEODORE MARTIN (1917-). Born, Syracuse, New York; student, University of Notre Dame, Notre Dame, Indiana, 1934-37; Ph.B., Gregorian University, Rome, Italy, 1940; S.T.L., Holy Cross College, Washington, D.C., 1943; S.T.D., Catholic University of America, Washington, D.C., 1945; entered Order of the Congregation of Holy Cross, Notre Dame, Indiana, 1934; ordained to priesthood, 1943; assistant professor of religion, University of Notre Dame, and head of department of religion, 1948-49; executive vice president, University of Notre Dame, 1949-52; president, 1952- ; fellow, American Academy of Arts and Sciences; Medal of Freedom, 1964; member, United States Commission on Civil Rights; chairman, 1969; member, Carnegie Commission on the Future of Higher Education; board of trustees, Rockefeller Foundation; United Negro College Fund, Inc.; Eleanor Roosevelt Memorial Foundation; and Carnegie Foundation for the Advancement of Teaching; board of directors, American Council on Education; Freedoms Foundation at Valley Forge; Education Development Center; member, President's General Advisory Committee on Foreign Assistance Programs; President's Commission on an All-Volunteer Armed Force; author of many books, including *God and the World of Man*, 1950; *Patterns for Educational Growth*, 1958; *Thoughts for Our Times*, 1962; *More Thoughts for Our Times*, 1965. (See also *Current Biography: January 1955*.)

HOWARD, JOHN A. (1921-). Born, Winnetka, Illinois; B.S., Northwestern University, 1947; M.A., 1949; Ph.D., 1962; served in First Infantry Division, 1942-45; awarded two Silver Stars and two Purple Hearts; instructor of French, Palos Verdes College, Rolling Hills, California, 1947-49; dean of students, 1949-51; vice president, 1950-51; president, 1951-55; president, Rockford College, 1960- ; first vice president, American Association of Presidents of Independent Colleges and Universities, 1968; president, 1969, 1970; member, board of trustees, The Philadelphia Society, 1968- ; executive vice chairman, President's Committee on Government Contracts, 1956-57; member, President's Commission on Presidential Scholars, 1969-   ; White House Task Force on Priorities in Higher Education, 1969-70; President's Commission on Marijuana and Drug Abuse, 1971-   ; National Council of Scholars, 1969-   ; (Illinois) Governor's Advisory Council, 1969-   ; recipient, Horatio Alger Award, 1967.

MOYNIHAN, DANIEL P. (1927-   ). Born, Tulsa, Oklahoma; B.A., Tufts University, cum laude, 1948; M.A., 1949; Ph.D., Fletcher School of Law and Diplomacy, 1961; Doctor of Laws, St. Louis University, 1968; Fulbright fellow, London (England) School of Economics and Political Science, 1950; special assistant to United States Secretary of Labor, 1961-62; executive assistant to Secretary, 1962-63; Assistant Secretary of Labor, 1963-65; director, Joint Center Urban Studies, Massachusetts Institute of Technology and Harvard University, 1966-   ; professor, education and urban politics, senior member, Kennedy School of Government, Harvard University, 1966-   ; assistant for urban affairs to President of United States, 1969-70; served with USNR, 1944-47; member, American Academy of Arts and Sciences; numerous committees, including New York State Democratic Convention, 1958-60; member, New York state delegation, Democratic National Convention, 1960; author, *Maximum Feasible Misunderstanding*, 1969; *Beyond the Melting Pot* (with Nathan Glazer), 1963. (See also *Current Biography: February 1968*.)

MURPHY, PATRICK V. (1920-   ). Born, Brooklyn, New York; B.A., St. John's University, New York City, 1954; Master of Public Administration, The City College of New York, 1960; graduate, National Law Enforcement Academy, Federal Bureau of Investigation, 1957; patrolman, New York City Police Department, 1963; commanding officer, Police Academy, 1964; assistant director, Office of Law Enforcement Assistance, United States Department of Justice, 1965-67; first public safety director, District of Columbia, 1967; first administrator, Law Enforcement Administration, 1968; commissioner, Detroit Police Department, 1970; 29th police commissioner, City of New York, 1970-   ; lieutenant (senior grade) World War II; member, Beta Gamma Sigma, national honor fraternity of business and public administration; charter member, past president, member of board of governors, Academy of Police Science; adviser to National Crime Commission on Civil Disorders, and the National Commission on the Causes and Prevention of Violence; vice chairman, Organized Crime Committee, International Association of Chiefs of Police.

NIXON, RICHARD M. (1913-). Born, Yorba Linda, California; A.B., Whittier College, 1934; LL.B., Duke University, 1937; practiced law, Whittier, California, 1937-41; attorney with Office of Emergency Management, Washington, D.C., 1942; lieutenant commander, United States Navy, 1942-46; United States House of Representatives (Republican, California), 1947-51; United States Senate, 1951-53; Vice President of the United States, 1952-60; Republican candidate for President, 1960; resumed law practice, Los Angeles, 1961; New York, 1963-68; President of the United States, 1968- ; author, *Six Crises,* 1962. (See also *Current Biography: December 1969.*)

PETERSON, MARTHA E. (1916-). Born, Jamestown, Kansas; A.B., University of Kansas, 1937; M.A., 1943; Ph.D., 1959; high school teacher in Kansas, 1937-42; instructor, University of Kansas, 1942-46; assistant dean of women, 1946-52; dean of women, 1952-56; dean of women, University of Wisconsin, 1956-63; assistant to the president, 1963; university dean of students, 1963-67; president, Barnard College, also dean in Columbia University, New York City, 1967- ; member, board of trustees, Chatham College, Pittsburgh, 1965- ; member, American Council on Education; member of executive board, National Association of Women Deans and Counselors, 1959-61; president, 1965-67. (See also *Current Biography: February 1969.*)

WALKER, HAROLD BLAKE (1904-). Born, Denver, Colorado; A.B., University of Denver, 1925; A.M., Boston University, 1927; B.D., McCormick Theological Seminary, 1932; honorary degrees from Emporia College, Hamilton College, University of Denver, Lake Forest College, Northwestern University, and National College of Education; pastor, Fullerton-Covenant Presbyterian Church, Chicago; First Presbyterian Church, Utica, New York; First Presbyterian Church, Oklahoma City; First Presbyterian Church, Evanston, Illinois; president, board of directors, McCormick Theological Seminary, Chicago, 1953-55; syndicated column, Chicago *Tribune*-New York *News,* 1954- ; president, director,

National Presbyterian Church and Center, Washington, D.C.; consultant, W. Clement Stone Enterprises, 1970- ; Freedoms Foundation Sermon Prize, 1950, 1956, 1962; Distinguished Citizenship Award, Denver, Colorado, 1958; author, *Going God's Way*, 1946; *Upper Room on Main Street*, 1954; *Thoughts to Live By*, 1965; *Prayers to Live By*, 1966; *Inspirational Thoughts for Every Day*, 1970; and many others; contributor to newspapers and religious publications.

WATSON, THOMAS J, JR. (1914-). Born, Dayton, Ohio; B.A., Brown University, 1937; International Business Machines Corporation, 1937-40, 1946- ; president, 1952-61; director, chairman of the board, 1961- ; United States Air Force, 1940-45, discharged with rating of senior pilot and rank of lieutenant colonel; member, National Executive Board, Boy Scouts of America; Citizen Regent, Smithsonian Institution; director, Bankers Trust Company (New York.); trustee, Air Force Aid Society, Brown University, California Institute of Technology, Colby College, Eisenhower Exchange Fellowships, Inc., The Rockefeller Foundation; recipient, Presidential Medal of Freedom; Air Medal.

AUTHOR INDEX: 1970-1971

A cumulative author index to the volumes of REPRESENTATIVE AMERICAN SPEECHES for the years 1937-1938 through 1959-1960 appears in the 1959-1960 volume and for the years 1960-1961 through 1969-1970 in the 1969-1970 volume.

153